Voice Mail- 703 790-2054
FAX 703-777-9096 (handwritten)

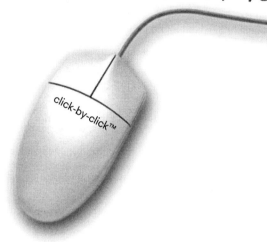

click-by-click™

Denise & Doug Reynolds

THE FRANKLIN PRESS, INC.

This book is not authorized, sponsored by, or affiliated with Quixtar, Inc. or Quixtar Investments, Inc. QUIXTAR.com is a service mark of Quixtar Investments, Inc.

click-by-click, inc. and the authors have attempted throughout the book to distinguish proprietary trademarks and service marks from descriptive terms by following the capitalization and style used by the owner of the marks. We cannot attest to the accuracy of this information. Use of a term in this book should not be regarded as affecting the validity of any trademark or service mark.

Engaging in the Quixtar business for profit has risk. Readers who engage in the Quixtar business opportunity for profit do so at their own risk, and the use of the information or techniques discussed in this book will not guarantee any particular financial performance or results. click-by-click, inc. and the authors expressly disclaim any liability, loss or risk, personal or otherwise, which is incurred as a result of the use and application of information contained in this book.

Information contained herein has been acquired from sources believed to be reliable. However, the authors and click-by-click, inc. in no way warrant or guarantee the accuracy or completeness of any information and are not responsible for any errors or omissions from the use of any information contained herein. QUIXTAR.com℠ is an ever changing and dynamic website, which may contain changes since the publication date of this book.

This publication is designed to provide accurate and correct information in regard to the subject matter covered. However, this book is sold and published with the understanding that the authors and publisher are not herein engaged in rendering legal, accounting or any other professional services. If such advice is needed, a qualified professional should be consulted.

Certain screen shots reproduced herein from the QUIXTAR.com℠ website for instructional purposes may be ©1999-2000 Quixtar, Inc. Screen captures in this book were done on March 21, 2000.

Important: click-by-click, inc. cannot provide software support. Please contact the appropriate software manufacturers' technical support line or Website for assistance.

Printed in the United States of America

Published by click-by-click, inc.
P.O. Box 11600
Fort Lauderdale, Florida 33339

ISBN: 0-9679347-0-2

Library of Congress Catalog Card Number: 00-190292

Printing Number   10 9 8 7 6 5 4 3 2 1

To William and Christina,
the future belongs to the Net Generation.

ABOUT THE AUTHORS

Denise & Doug Reynolds live in sunny Fort Lauderdale, Florida, with their two children, William & Christina, and their Shih Tzu guard dog, Jabbers. Graduates of the University of Virginia, Doug & Denise are independent business owners who divide their time between their keyboards and the people and activities that matter most in their lives.

ACKNOWLEDGEMENTS

To our parents, Don & Ethel Bates, for their unconditional support for all our endeavors, and Joe & Sarah Hrubik, for their steadfast faith and example.

To Tim & Connie Foley, Bob & Tamie Newmeyer, and Bert & Marie Oliver, for their friendship, their vision, and their leadership.

To Laurie Geronemus, a gifted writer and friend, for her sensitive editing and proofing of the original manuscript and her encouragement each step of the way.

TABLE OF CONTENTS

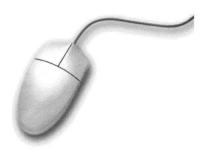

CLICK 1   WELCOME TO QUIXTAR......................... 1
                SO WHAT'S QUIXTAR 1
                MAKING YOUR LIFE BETTER 2

CLICK 2   MAKE YOURSELF AT HOME...................... 3
                THE HOME OF YOUR DREAMS 3
                THE RIGHT ADDRESS...............................4
                YOUR FRONT DOOR.................................6
                YOUR SET OF KEYS 7
                KNOCK, KNOCK, WHO'S THERE?...................7
                CLIENT REGISTRATION 8
                INTERNATIONAL VISITORS........................ 10
                QUIXTAR HOTSPOTS............................. 11
                SHOPPING DIRECTORY 12
                RETURNING HOME 15

CLICK 3   AT YOUR SERVICE 16
                HOW QUIXTAR WORKS........................... 16
                HELP FAQS 16
                NAVIGATION TIPS................................ 17
                SEARCH TIPS 18

TABLE OF CONTENTS

SITE MAP 18
PLACING AN ORDER 19
ABOUT US.. 19
ABOUT MY ORDER 21
FORGOT PASSWORD 21
CONTACT US... 21
EDIT PROFILE.. 22

CLICK 4   LET'S GO SHOPPING 23
SHOPPING A BETTER MOUSETRAP 23
THE SEVEN TYPES OF SHOPPERS 24
SHOPPING CARTS 28
QUIXTAR EXCLUSIVES 30
HOT BUYS.. 30
STORE FOR MORE 30
PARTNER STORES 31

CLICK 5   MY HOME 32
WHAT'S NEW 32
SPECIAL OFFERS 32
EXPERT ADVICE 33
MY ASSESSMENT 34
CLEAN IT UP 35
WATER WATCH 36
COOKING CLUB..................................... 36
GO SHOPPING 36
SHOPPING CART.................................... 38
HOME SERVICES 42

CLICK 6   MY HEALTH...................................... 43
WHAT'S NEW 43
SPECIAL OFFERS 44
EXPERT ADVICE 45
MY ASSESSMENT................................... 45

TABLE OF CONTENTS

REFERENCE DESK 46
GO SHOPPING 47

CLICK 7   MY SELF 49
WHAT'S NEW 49
SPECIAL OFFERS 50
EXPERT ADVICE 51
MY ASSESSMENT 51
VIRTUAL LOOK 52
GO SHOPPING 56

CLICK 8   HOT BUYS 59
REAL DEALS 59

CLICK 9   STORE FOR MORE℠ 63
YOUR FAVORITE STORE 63
FASHION 65
CONVENIENCE 66
ELECTRONICS....................................... 66
HOME 67
SEASONAL... 67
HOT BUYS 68
GET CATALOG 68
CUSTOMER SERVICE 69
SFM HOME PAGE 69
SHOPPING CART.................................... 69

CLICK 10 PARTNER STORES 71
SHOPPING SHORTCUTS 71
QUICK LIST 75
HOW IT WORKS.................................... 81
SPECIAL OFFERS 82
REWARDS BROCHURE 83

TABLE OF CONTENTS

WHAT'S NEW 83

CLICK 11   CATALOG CITY 84
   WELCOME TO CATALOG CITY 84
   PRODUCTS 86
   CATALOGS 88
   SEARCH 91
   A-Z INDEX 92

CLICK 12   MY QUIXTAR 132
   YOUR PERSONALIZED WEB PAGE 132
   EDIT PROFILE 133
   HEADLINE NEWS 134
   QUIXTAR NEWS 135
   MAPS 135
   STOCK QUOTES 136
   WEATHER 137
   NETWORK SAVINGS PARTNERS 137
   PV/BV PROFILE 138
   MEMBER REWARDS 139

CLICK 13   MEMBER PERKS 140
   INTRO TO PERKS 140
   MEMBER PRICING 141
   MEMBER REWARDS 142
   MY QUIXTAR 142
   NETWORK SAVINGS 142
   ARE YOU READY 143
   REGISTER NOW 143
   PRIVACY POLICY 144
   REDEMPTION CENTER 144
   Q CREDIT RULES 146

TABLE OF CONTENTS

CLICK 14　INCOME OPTIONS 147
　　　　　EXTRA INCOME 147
　　　　　IBO REGISTRATION 148
　　　　　PRIVACY POLICY................................ 150

CLICK 15　VIRTUAL OFFICE 152
　　　　　VIRTUAL OFFICE TOUR 152
　　　　　WHAT'S NEW 153
　　　　　SERVICES 154
　　　　　EDIT PROFILE.................................... 154
　　　　　LOGOUT 155

CLICK 16　PRODUCT ORDERING 156
　　　　　QUICK ORDER 157
　　　　　DITTO DELIVERY℠ – THE BASICS............... 158
　　　　　DITTO DELIVERY℠ – THE BEST PART.......... 163
　　　　　DITTO DELIVERY℠ – THE DETAILS............. 164
　　　　　MARKETING TIPS................................. 165
　　　　　MEETING SUPPORT 165

CLICK 17　MY BUSINESS 167
　　　　　RENEW 168
　　　　　REWARDS & INCENTIVES 168
　　　　　MY ORGANIZATION 169
　　　　　PV/BV... 172

INDEX 177

Introduction

The launch of the QUIXTAR.com^{SM} Web site on 9.1.99 marked a historic day in the world of e-commerce. Experiencing over 20 million hits on opening day, the site rose to the top 5 e-commerce sites on the Web during its first two weeks. Imagine visiting a new shopping spot that had several "million-dollar" sales days in its first month of business. That would be one hot shopping spot!

QUIXTAR.com^{SM} is much more than a new shopping mall. It's a unique tri-digital destination offering something for everyone - Independent Business Owners, Members and Clients. MICROSOFT® and IBM® were key technology partners in the creation of QUIXTAR.com^{SM}, along with FRY MULTIMEDIA and C-E COMMUNICATIONS' digital solutions group, tdah!. The site contains over 15,000 pages and over 100,000 links. It's big, very big. But it's also very personal.

How personal is it? Very personal. Ladies who use the **Virtual Face** feature will receive customized recommendations for their cosmetics when they answer questions about the color of their eyes, skin and hair and the shape of their face, eyes and lips. All without having to face the high-pressure that often accompanies such personalized recommendations at the cosmetic counters found in the department stores of a traditional mall.

More personalized recommendations are available on the site in the sections called **My Home**, **My Health** and **My Self** for anyone who completes a short multiple-choice profile called **My Assessment**. You can even design a customized program to supply your household with whatever routine consumable items you need. Features like these give a whole new meaning to the concept of personal service.

Something For Everyone

Whether you visit QUIXTAR.com^{SM} as an IBO (Independent Business Owner), Member, or Client, you will find lots of exciting opportunities await you. In addition to offering good deals on the products and services we need for today's busy lifestyles,

QUIXTAR.com℠ gives you the gift of time. Take the time you used to spend running around town to pick-up all your stuff and get that time back, to spend with the people and activities that matter most to you.

QUIXTAR.com℠ merchant Partner Stores are eager to serve the millions of people who visit the site. They will deliver the things you need directly to your door. Let your fingers do the clicking and save the running around for delivery services like UPS.

HOW TO USE THIS BOOK

This book will introduce you to the QUIXTAR.com℠ site, click-by-click™. Take a guided tour through the highlights of the site from the comfort of your favorite easy chair. Then, head over to your keyboard, login, and take yourself out for a ride on the QUIXTAR.com℠ site. Once you get past the first few clicks, jump around to whichever section interests you most.

SPECIAL ICONS

Special icons appear throughout this book to point out tips and tricks that will make you into an expert before you know it.

 These boxes give you insider tips that make it easier to use the Quixtar site. These tips will allow you to move through the site more quickly. They will be your shortcuts to save you time while you navigate the site.

 These boxes highlight words you will run across on the site that may be new to you. Refer back to these boxes when you encounter an unfamiliar word. Use these definitions to brush up on your computer lingo and impress your children with your new vocabulary.

 These boxes will keep you pointed toward your goals. They will show you how to make the most of your Quixtar experience by increasing your volume or your Q-credits. Smart shoppers welcome a suggestion from a friend. We're here to help.

WHAT TO DO WHEN

You'll also find special text to lead you through the site, click-by-click™:

What you type	Things you type will be shown in bold, blue color print.
Press Enter	Any keys you press or items you select with your mouse will be shown in blue color print.
On-screen text	Any messages or text you see on your screen will appear in bold print.

SITE UPDATES

The good news about making the Web a part of your life, is that Web sites are dynamic, and ever changing. This is a good thing because you'll always get the latest information, and the hottest deals. On the other hand, change can be a bit frustrating at times. Like if you are following a guide, click-by-click™, and your screen appears differently than it's described in the book. Don't worry! Any changes you notice will be changes for the better. And you've got a great **Customer Service** team to help you iron out any little questions you encounter along the way.

TRADEMARKS

We have appropriately capitalized all terms in this book that are known to be trademarks. We cannot attest to the accuracy of this information. Use of a term in this book should not be considered as affecting the validity of any trademark or service mark.

QUIXTAR is a registered trademark of Quixtar Investments, Incorporated.
MICROSOFT® INTERNET EXPLORER is a registered trademark of Microsoft Corporation.
NETSCAPE NAVIGATOR® is a registered trademark of Netscape Communications Corporation.
Screen reproductions in this book were created using the program Collage Complete from Inner Media, Inc., Hollis, NH.

CLICK 1

WELCOME TO QUIXTAR

> *CLICK HERE TO FIND OUT WHAT ALL THE HOOPLA'S ABOUT. YOU'LL DISCOVER A WHOLE NEW WAY OF GETTING THE THINGS YOU WANT. CREATE MORE TIME IN YOUR SCHEDULE. REDUCE YOUR CHORES. AND YOUR STRESS. MAKE YOUR LIFE BETTER. IT'S ALL WITHIN YOUR REACH. WHY DIDN'T SOMEBODY THINK OF THIS BEFORE?*

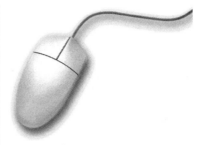

WELCOME TO QUIXTAR

SO WHAT'S QUIXTAR

QUIXTAR.com℠ is the greatest thing since sliced bread. Really, it is. Remember, back in the old days when you had to slice off a piece of bread with a knife every time you wanted to make yourself a sandwich or a piece of toast? It took more time, was messy, and even a little bit dangerous. When sliced bread came out, it was a big improvement. No mess, no wasted slices, and no sharp objects for little hands to handle. And it was still fresh. Good quality. And convenient.

Some day, we'll all look back at the traditional way of shopping and wonder why we ever shopped that way. Dragging ourselves and our children from store to store. Fighting for parking spaces. In the rain, or the snow. Spending our precious free time pulling stuff off the shelves, loading up our baskets, standing in line, and lugging it back home again.

We think you'll agree that you've got better things to do with your time than standing in line. But until lately, you probably haven't had much of a choice. Every home needs to be stocked with food, clothing, and all of life's little essentials. It's not a particularly fun job, but somebody has to do it.

But that somebody no longer has to be you. Now, you've got a choice. Let somebody else do the running around. Bring the stuff you need right to your door. You won't even have to lift a finger. Well, maybe just one finger. Your index finger. The one you use to click on the mouse that lives beside your computer. Or the one you use to operate your remote control, if you use WebTV®.

When you realize that you can get virtually everything you need, from the comfort and convenience of your own home, we think you'll agree that QUIXTAR.com℠ is the greatest thing to come along since sliced bread.

MAKING YOUR LIFE BETTER

Just like sliced bread made peoples' lives better when it was first introduced, QUIXTAR.com℠ can make your life better, too. This Internet-based business delivers the power of the Web to make your life easier and better. Not only can you save time by shopping from its hundreds of stores. You can save money, too. Just by shopping from home. And you can even use this site to earn extra money. A little, or a lot. It's up to you.

Come along with us as we guide you through the wonders of this incredible site, click-by-click™. Once you experience this revolution in shopping, benefits, and business ownership, we're confident that you'll agree, the old way of shopping is just about as appealing as a piece of stale bread.

CLICK 2   MAKE YOURSELF AT HOME

CLICK HERE TO BEGIN YOUR QUIXTAR EXPERIENCE. LOG IN AS A GUEST AND EXPLORE ALL THE FABULOUS SHOPPING ADVENTURES THAT AWAIT YOU. CHECK OUT THE BENEFITS OF MEMBERSHIP. OR BECOME AN IBO & CASH IN ON THE DIGITAL REVOLUTION. DO QUIXTAR ANY WAY YOU WANT. YOU'RE GOING TO LOVE IT!

MAKE YOURSELF AT HOME

THE HOME OF YOUR DREAMS

Welcome home! There's no place like home. Home, sweet home. Home is where the heart is. When you stop to think about it, home conjures up some pretty strong images in our minds. Whether our childhood memories of home are warm and wonderful, or not, we all have the opportunity, as adults, to create the home environment we want.

So, what'll it be? A tidy little bungalow? A city condo? A suburban family home? A home in the mountains, or in the country? A cabin on the lake? A mansion on the beach?

Wherever you choose to call home, it should be a special place. A place where you can kick back and relax. Walk around in your underwear, if you want. A place that feels comfortable. Friendly. Welcoming. A place you can call your own.

How about a second home? Not the brick and mortar kind. Not another rent or mortgage payment. We're talking about an online home. A place you can go, whenever you want. A warm and friendly place. Where you always feel welcome.

QUIXTAR.com℠ can be your home away from home. Or your home within a home. Your online home. Millions of people have already found it to be a very special place. We think you will, too.

THE RIGHT ADDRESS

Before you go out to visit a good friend who's just moved into a new home, chances are you'll give them a call to be sure you know their new address. They'll probably give you some directions, so you can find them easily. So, let's take a minute to verify the QUIXTAR site address and be sure you know how to get there.

Remember the first time you drove a car? It was a little bit scary. But it was so exciting! And you didn't have to learn all by yourself. You had someone there, right beside you, to encourage you and help you along.

Getting around on the Internet is a lot like driving on a highway. You'll need a good, reliable vehicle to get you from place to place. Your vehicle is called a browser.

Browser A special software program that lets you get around on the Internet. It includes extra features to enhance your experience, like the ability to bookmark your favorite spots and a history feature to help you get back to the places you've visited recently. Most computers come with built-in browsers, like Netscape Navigator® and Microsoft® Internet Explorer.

Just like the vehicle in your garage needs power to go anywhere, your browser needs power to take you from place to place. That power is available from an Internet Service Provider, or ISP for short. They'll provide you with this power through an online connection. Today, most people connect to their ISPs using a regular telephone line. Faster, high-speed connections are also available for an additional fee.

ISP An Internet Service Provider provides you with a connection to the Internet, much like a power company provides you with a connection to electrical power. Most people today connect to their ISP using a regular telephone line, which dials the ISP's number and connects you to their computer system, which is already connected to the Internet.

If you don't have an online connection yet, don't worry. You can use your existing telephone line to connect to the Internet once you set-up an account with an ISP. Grab a buddy who's already online and ask them to help you get wired. It's quick. And painless.

Okay, so now you're online and ready to visit the Quixtar site. Start up your browser and let's go! Look at the top of your screen and find the address box. This is where you'll type in the address you want to visit. Sometimes this box will have the letters URL in front of it.

URL An acronym for Uniform Resource Locator, a URL is nothing more than an address that your browser uses to locate the site you want to visit. The URL for Quixtar is **www.quixtar.com**.

Go ahead and click in the address box on your screen and type in **www.quixtar.com**. Now, press the Enter key on your keyboard. Watch as your browser drives you right to the front door of the Quixtar site!

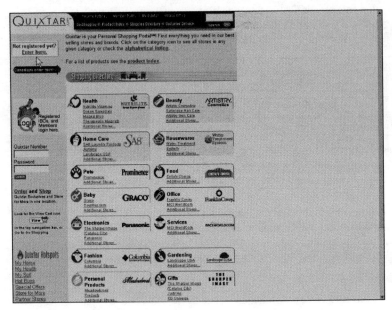

FIGURE 2-1   QUIXTAR HOME PAGE

YOUR FRONT DOOR

Just like your actual home, QUIXTAR.com℠ has a front door. It's the first thing you see when you arrive at their address. Some people call this a Home Page. They call it a portal. The only difference between a door and a portal is the size and impressiveness of it. A portal is an especially grand door, or entrance to a home. And grand it is! So, we'll call it a portal. Your Personal Shopping Portal℠. When you enter here, you'll find everything you need. Friendly people. Great advice. Lots of your favorite stores and brands. But this door leads to more than just great shopping. You'll see. It could be the key to the home of your dreams.

YOUR SET OF KEYS

To get inside this new home, you'll need a set of keys. These keys will be unique to you. Nobody else will have the same set of keys that you do. And that's important. Because, like the keys to your home, these keys provide you with security.

You'll have two keys to this place. One is called a Quixtar number. And the other is called a password. We'll tell you where to get them in a little while. For now, just remember to keep your keys with you at all times. And don't give them out to strangers. You may decide to share your first key with some close friends. But the password is just for you.

KNOCK, KNOCK, WHO'S THERE?

When you first knock at the door of QUIXTAR.com℠, you'll be asked for your keys. If you don't have them yet, don't worry. It's easy to get some. Look on the left side of your screen and find the red words **Not registered yet? Enter here.** It's okay, go ahead and click on Enter Here. We're here to guide you through your new home, click-by-click™. So relax. We won't let anything scary happen to you.

The next page you'll see is **Not Registered Yet?** Take a look at the three ways you can "do" Quixtar. One of them will be just right for you. You could become a Member. Members have special privileges. Click on To Register as a New Quixtar Member – Click Here to pick up a set of keys designed just for Members.

Check out the benefits of ownership by clicking on To Register as a New Quixtar Affiliated Independent Business Owner – Click Here. Everyone knows the owners always get the best deals. Maybe you'd like to be an Independent Business Owner, or IBO for short. You'll get a set of keys that allow you to take full advantage of every feature of this place.

Or, perhaps you'd feel more comfortable just being a guest. That's okay. Guests can shop at all the same great places as Members and IBOs. Being a guest is very convenient. You'll get all your purchases delivered to your door. With great guarantees. Click on To Register as a New Quixtar Client – Click Here if you'd

like to pick up a set of keys designed just for guests. You don't
have to register yet. You can browse through the shops on the
site all you like. Until you see something you want to buy, or click
to enter a Partner Store. Then you'll be led to a screen where you
can register and receive your special guest keys.

FIGURE 2-2   NOT REGISTERED YET?

CLIENT REGISTRATION

If you've decided to shop as a guest, you'll be given a set of keys
reserved for special Clients. There's a short application to
complete. But registration is *free*. And you won't have to retype
your shipping address and that kind of stuff each time you return.

On the **Not Registered Yet?** screen, point your mouse cursor at
the words To Become a Quixtar Client – Register Now and click.
Now you'll see a **Client Registration** page.

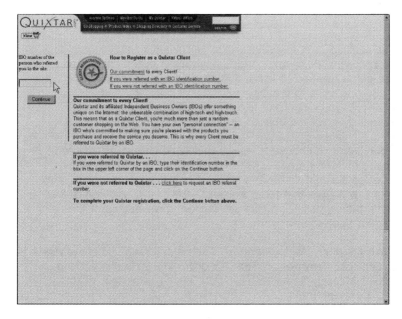

FIGURE 2-3   CLIENT REGISTRATION

Go ahead and point your mouse cursor at the first box, click in the box and type in the **Quixtar #** of the person who referred you to the site. Next you'll see a short registration form. Begin by clicking in the first box and type in your **Name**. Point and click in each box until you've typed in the correct information. If you make a mistake, don't worry. Just click in that box again and press the Delete key on your keyboard. Then type it in the way you want it.

The last thing you'll type in is your choice of key. The first key will be provided for you, but you get to pick out your second key. This key is your password. It can be anywhere from 6 to 15 characters long. You can choose letters, numbers, or a combination of the two. Spaces cannot be used.

Click in the **Password** box and type in your choice of **password**. Then, click in the next box and retype your same password. This makes sure you get exactly the key you want. Now, just in case you forget your password, and lock yourself out of this place, you're going to need to leave a spare key with a friend. The way that you do this is to create a secret hint question and answer. That way, if you ever forget, a friendly **Customer Service** representative will be able to remind you.

You may want to choose a **Password Hint Question** like your mother's maiden name, or where you were born. Whatever you choose, be sure you'll always remember the answer! Okay, now type in the **Password Hint Answer**. Check the spelling to be sure it's just right. Then click on the Continue button at the bottom of your screen.

Congratulations! You've done it. The next screen will show you your **Quixtar Number**. Write this down in a safe place. In a couple of places. Now you have both keys to the door of this place. Come on in!

INTERNATIONAL VISITORS

It's always exciting to have visitors from another country. They add a different perspective to our lives. We are enriched by their presence. You'll be sharing this special site with visitors just like these. Even though QUIXTAR.com℠ is based in the United States, it does reside on the World Wide Web so everyone, anywhere on the planet, can take a look at QUIXTAR.com℠.

For now, registrations are limited to people residing in the U.S. and Canada. Canadian visitors will click on Canadians enter here! when they come to the front door. There's a Canadian red maple leaf right there to mark the spot. Once inside the Canadian site, the navigation works much the same as in the U.S. site.

And who knows, registrations may open up to residents of other countries in the future. Check back every now and then for updates on other locations.

QUIXTAR HOTSPOTS

If you're like us, you keep a little stash of things that are really important to you right inside your front door. Things like your keys, your wallet, your umbrella. Things you use often, and don't want to have to go hunt around for. You'll be glad to know that the things you use most are kept handy here, too. Right inside the front door. They're called **Quixtar Hotspots**.

These **Hotspots** are links to the parts of the site you'll return to again and again. And putting them right up front saves you from having to look for them. Especially when you're in a hurry.

To get to a **Hotspot**, just click on the arrow in the drop-down box and highlight the place you want to go with your mouse. Then click, and you're there! **Hotspots** include links to the most popular shopping destinations like **Quixtar Exclusives, My Home, My Health, My Self, Hot Buys, Special Offers, Store For More**, and **Partner Stores**. There are also links here to **View Quixtar Intro, Site Map, Tips and Tricks, Privacy Policy** and **Terms of Use**.

Explore these at your leisure. You'll find each of these areas covered, click-by-click™, later on in this guide. We'd suggest starting out by clicking on View Quixtar Intro. This is a short, fast-moving video presentation about the site. You'll need a special add-in piece of software to view it. Don't worry. If your computer doesn't already have this, you'll have a chance to download it for free. Enjoy the show!

Another area you might like to visit now is **Tips and Tricks**. This will give you a few pointers on how the site works.

IBOs will have a separate section at their front door called **More Hotspots**. This drop-down shortcut list works the same way. It includes links to some of your favorite places, like **Ditto Delivery, Income Options, Member Perks, What's New, My Business, Online Survey, Site Status, Quixtar Intro, Site Map, Tips and Tricks, Privacy Policy** and **Terms of Use**. We'll talk about each of these areas, in click-by-click™ detail, later on in this guide.

Click on Site Status for the latest news on improvements that have
been made to the site. And don't forget to click on Online Survey
to voice your opinion on the site's features. You'd be surprised
how many enhancements are made to the site as a result of
feedback received through this survey.

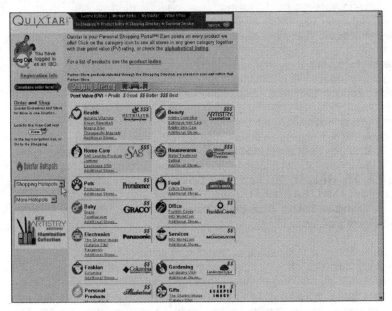

FIGURE 2-4   SHOPPING DIRECTORY WITH HOTSPOTS

SHOPPING DIRECTORY

Have you ever been traveling away from your hometown, and
needed to stop at a mall to pick something up? After you parked
your car and went inside, chances are, the first thing you looked
for was a **Shopping Directory**. One of those large illuminated
signs that are located inside the mall. The ones that show all the
stores, by category, and assign each one if them a tiny little
number. Once you locate the big red "You Are Here" X on the
sign, you look over the directory to see which stores they have
and decide where you want to go.

If you can find your way around a mall using one of those hard-to-read shopping directories, then finding your way around this shopping site will be a snap. There are no little numbers to decipher, no long aisles to walk, and no wandering around trying to find the directory itself. Here, your **Shopping Directory** is right at your front door.

You'll see easy to understand **Categories**, like **Health, Beauty, Home Care, Housewares, Pets, Food, Baby, Office, Electronics, Services, Fashion, Gardening, Personal Products, Gifts, Leisure, Toys, Sports** and **Automotive**. Each Category has a cute little icon next to it that you can click on. And when you do, you'll see a list of all the stores in that category. Choose the store you'd like to visit, click on it, and whoosh, you're there. No long walk to find the escalator.

What's Behind Door Number Two? If you don't see the store you're looking for, click on **Catalog City**. They have their own **A-Z Index** of hundreds of shops. And only a few of them are included in the **Shopping Directory** up front. When the **Shopping Directory** leads you to a **Catalog City** page, follow the link to their website and then use the **Catalog City A-Z Index** to get to the shop you want.

You'll notice that each **Category** on the **Shopping Directory** has a few popular shops or brands listed just below it. If any of these are the ones you want, great. Just click on the name shown here and you'll go right to that section. If any of these featured places are unfamiliar to you, these might be good places to browse through, so you can see why they're so popular.

Watch Out for Those Flashing Red Signs
IBOs will see a special feature on their **Shopping Directory** – flashing red dollar signs! These call your attention to the places where you'll earn the most points (PV) while you shop.   The more dollar signs, the better the points, so go shopping at these spots first!

Some of the links in the **Shopping Directory** will take you to an item from a featured brand. When we clicked on Columbia®, in the **Fashion** category, we found a cozy, plaid shirt that looked warm and inviting. But we wondered if there were any other fashion items made by Columbia®. So, we went up to the navy blue navigational bar, at the top of the screen, clicked in the Search box and typed in **Columbia**. And sure enough, we found more Columbia® Sportswear items. So, remember, you're not limited to the first thing you see!

Perhaps you'd rather not use a shopping directory at all. Some people would rather go to the information desk at a new mall and ask for a certain store by name. If that's your preference, you can click on alphabetical listing, shown in red just above the **Shopping Directory**. At the top of this page, you'll see each letter of the alphabet. Click on a letter and you'll go right to a list of all the shops that begin with that letter. Now, pick the one you want, click on it and you're there. Or, you can use your scroll bar to see all the shops and brands that are listed.

If you're the kind of shopper who knows exactly what you want and you'd like a quick order experience, click on the red Order link, located just above the **Hotspots** on the front page.   You'll go right to your **Shopping Cart** where you can **Add an item** by entering the **Quantity** and **SKU**.   If you'd like to enter a bunch of items at once, click on Multi-Line Form. Now, enter all the items you need and then click on Add to Cart.

Or maybe you're looking for a specific item, but you're not sure which stores might carry it. You'll like the **product index**. Click on product index, shown in red just above the **Shopping Directory**. At the top of this page, you'll see each letter of the alphabet. Click on a letter and you'll go right to a list of all the products that begin with that letter. Now, pick the one you want, click on it and you're there. Or, you can use your scroll bar to see all the products that are listed. One more click on the product you like will bring up a full page with the product description and an **Add** to Cart button.

Often, people who are very tight on time rely on the services of a personal shopper to locate just exactly what they want or need. If you'd like to have someone search the stores for you,

you'll appreciate the wonderful **Search** feature found on each page of the site.   Look at the top of your screen, in the navy blue navigational bar.   You'll see a white box.   Click in the box and type in the item you're looking for.   Type in a word or two, like **eye shadow**, and click on GO!   Now sit back and marvel at all the time you just saved.   You can even type in your favorite stock number and that will work, too.

For those of us who are tired of running out to the store to get the things we've just run out of, there's a special program designed just to eliminate that frustrated feeling.   It's called **Ditto Delivery**.   You'll find it in **Hotspots**, on the front page.   It's great for scheduling automatic deliveries of the things you use – and use up – most often.   Stuff like toothpaste, cereal, pantyhose, paper towels, pet food.   We love using this complimentary service, especially for stuff that's bulky, or heavy to carry.

If you're the kind of person who just enjoys browsing around to see what's available, you can click on the red Shop link, located just above the **Hotspots** on the front page.   You'll be led to the **Go Shopping** section of the site where you can shop by picture. We'll guide you through each one of these shopping methods, click-by-click™, later on in this guide.

RETURNING HOME

Whenever you want to return to the home page, just click on the big blue Q at the top left of your screen.   You'll find yourself back at your front door, right where you started.

CLICK 3

AT YOUR SERVICE

CLICK HERE TO VISIT SHELLIE, OSCAR, OR ANY QUIXTAR CUSTOMER SERVICE REPRESENTATIVE ONLINE, ANYTIME YOU NEED INFORMATION...ABOUT QUIXTAR...HOW QUIXTAR WORKS...QUESTIONS ABOUT YOUR ORDER...HOW TO CONTACT QUIXTAR...WHAT TO DO IF YOU FORGET YOUR PASSWORD OR HOW TO EDIT YOUR PROFILE.

CUSTOMER SERVICE

HOW QUIXTAR WORKS

If you have already viewed the **Tips & Tricks** on the Home Page and are still yearning for more specifics on how the site works, then you've come to the right place. In this section you will find **Help FAQ**, **Navigation Tips**, **Search Tips**, a **Site Map** and the details on **Placing An Order**.

HELP FAQS

If you have questions about **Getting Started, Password, Shopping, Profile, Ditto Delivery** and more, check out this section. Chances are, you'll find the answer right here.

FAQs An acronym for Frequently Asked Questions. Reading FAQs can be a time-saver for you and reduces the phone calls made to Customer Service. You'll find commonly asked questions and their answers right here. Aren't you glad to know someone already asked?

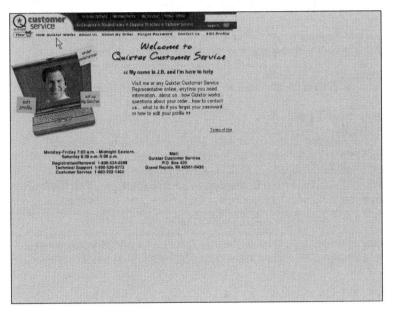

FIGURE 3-1   CUSTOMER SERVICE

NAVIGATION TIPS

So you know where you want to go but can't figure out how to get there? This section gives you a couple of ways to get started.

Let's say you're planning a trip to Disney World. You know that there's more than one right way to get there. You could travel major highways, choose the turnpike, or take the scenic drive. All of them would get you there but some ways are faster and some ways are more fun.

Just like planning out the route you'll drive to get to Disney World, you have many ways to get to where you want to go on the Quixtar site. Loosen up, relax, and try some different approaches. You'll find your favorite way. And remember to enjoy the trip!

Can't get in? Ever find yourself on the outside of a site and can't log-in? Try going in the "back-door", through **Customer Service**. You won't need a password & you'll be able to navigate quite a bit of the site. And of course, they'll be able to give you your password there!

SEARCH TIPS

Ever find yourself standing in line at one of those big discount stores wondering where to find something – and looking for someone to tell you where it is? Here's another Quixtar advantage. Instant help is always at your fingertips. The **Search** feature will take you to hundreds of places – and thousands of products – in just a few seconds.

This section tells you how to search the site to find exactly what you are looking for – by name, description or even stock number.

SITE MAP

Site Map A Site Map is exactly what you think it is – a visual layout of the site sections that shows you how they connect to each other. Just like seeing main roads & side streets on a road map, you'll see the main sections of the site & all of the smaller sections that branch off of them & how to get from one section to another.

PLACING AN ORDER

Want to learn how to shop for products? How to use the Shopping Cart? How to checkout? Explore your payment and shipping options? Have questions about international orders? Click on the links in this section and you'll become a professional Quixtar shopper in no time!

Links Usually shown in a different color and/or underlined on a Web page, links are a way of connecting text or pictures from one page to another. When you place your mouse pointer over a link you will see it change from an arrow to a hand pointing to the next page.

ABOUT US

Click here for **FAQs** about shopping at Quixtar. You'll find answers to questions about shopping, ordering, searching for products, credit card security, product in-stock status, shipping, canceling an order, returning merchandise, warranty and guarantee information, and Partner Stores.

The Quixtar Pledge is found here as well. It covers Quixtar's **Privacy Policy**, use of information you provide in your Personal Profile and online questionnaires such as **My Assessment** and **Ask an Expert**, optional receipt of promotional mailings, links to other sites, use of cookies, sharing of your information with third-parties (Not!), changing your personal information, contacting Quixtar, a business snapshot and transactional security.

Cookies A cookie is a small file sent to your computer by Quixtar to help identify you. This allows Quixtar to customize your Web experience to your personal needs. These cookies are safe – you can't get viruses from them & they aren't shared with anyone else.

SSL Encryption   Secure Sockets Layer encryption technology provides you with the highest level of security on the Internet. It scrambles your credit card number & purchase information so it can only be viewed by Quixtar. Your information is probably a lot more secure with Quixtar than with your local gas station attendant or restaurant cashier. So order with confidence knowing that your personal SSL guard is standing watch to protect you!

You can shop with confidence at Quixtar because they don't just guarantee their products' quality – they guarantee you'll be satisfied with them. Quixtar is made up of different stores and groups of stores. Each offers their own guarantee. Here are some of the guarantees you'll have when you purchase from Quixtar:

Quixtar Exclusives Store Guarantee   Quixtar stands behind the quality of their products & guarantees your satisfaction. If for any reason you are not completely satisfied with your purchase from the Exclusives Store, you may return it for an exchange or refund. (Limited guarantees apply to designated products.)

Store For More Guarantee   If for any reason you are not completely satisfied with your purchase from the Store For More, you may return it for an exchange or refund. Specific manufacturers' warranties are available for most mechanical devices purchased at the Store For More. In addition, Quixtar warrants the merchandise for a period of one full year from the date of original purchase or receipt as a gift.

Now That's Service!   Ever seen something you wanted to order – but didn't – because of the hassle and extra shipping involved if it had to go back? On **Quixtar Exclusives** merchandise, Quixtar takes all the risk out of it by sending you a Prepaid Postal Return Label for any merchandise returns. And on any exchanges, they let you keep the unwanted item until you receive its replacement – not like some places that bill you for the second shipment & don't credit you for the return until they receive it back.

Partner Store Guarantees   *The Quixtar guarantees shown above do not apply to products purchased from **Partner Stores**, which are covered under their own guarantees.*

ABOUT MY ORDER

Come here for answers to any questions you have about your order after it has been placed. Find information on **Returns & Exchanges** here or **View Order History** for orders you have placed.

FORGOT PASSWORD

Thank goodness Quixtar keeps track of your password. We have enough trouble remembering where we put our car keys! This is the spot to come to when you need a little reminder. Quixtar keeps a hint question and answer on file for you so they can tell you your password in case you forget it. Or they can email your password to the address you provided when you first registered.

CONTACT US

No matter how wonderful our computers are, sometimes you just want to talk to a real human being and Quixtar gives you that ability. Unlike some e-commerce sites that will only communicate with you via email, the folks at Quixtar recognize that high-tech is best when supported by high-touch. So go ahead, pick up the phone and speak to someone at one of Quixtar's toll-free numbers. Of course you can email or snail mail them if you prefer.

QuickTip

Toll-Free Phone Numbers   Here they are:
Registration/Renewal(US)   800-524-6588
Technical Support   800-529-8772
Customer Service   (US)   800-222-1462
Monday-Friday   7:00AM-Midnight EST
Saturday   8:30AM-5:00PM   EST
Canadian Registration   877-919-9865
Canadian Customer Service 800-436-3565

EDIT PROFILE

If you need to change your address, password, or personal profile information of any kind, this is the place to go. Here you'll access the customized information you've set-up in the **Shopping**, **My Quixtar**, **General**, and **Virtual Office** sections.

CLICK 4   LET'S GO SHOPPING

> *CLICK HERE TO EMBARK ON ONE OF THE MOST INCREDIBLE SHOPPING ADVENTURES AVAILABLE ON THE WEB! YOU'LL HAVE HUNDREDS OF STORES TO CHOOSE FROM AND YOU'LL NEVER GET SORE FEET FROM POUNDING THE PAVEMENT AT YOUR LOCAL MALL OR SUPERSTORE. WHETHER YOU NEED EVERYDAY HOUSEHOLD CONSUMABLES OR SPECIALTY GIFT ITEMS, YOU'LL FIND THEM THROUGH QUIXTAR.*

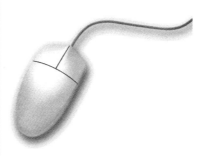

LET'S GO SHOPPING

A BETTER MOUSETRAP

How does that old saying go? Something like "build a better mousetrap and the world will make a pathway to your door". Well the person who came up with that saying was probably thinking about a gizmo to trap one of those pesky gray mice. But the mouse that lives happily on your desktop, alongside your computer, deserves something better, too, and so do you.

Today's hectic lifestyles leave most of us with too little time to get all the shopping and errands done and even less time for ourselves. Whether you live alone, or have a family to shop for, the last thing you want to do at the end of a busy day is run around town to get the stuff you need to buy.

Quixtar offers you an alternative shopping experience. Put on your favorite music, pour yourself a cup of coffee, put your feet up if you feel like it, and click your list away. Once you get the hang of it, you'll agree that this is a vastly superior shopping experience.

No restless children in tow, begging you to add things to your cart that you don't want or need. No fighting for the only parking space. No high-pressure salespeople. Help, when you need it, if you need it. No bags to lug home. No running through the rain or snow. You're going to love shopping the Quixtar way!

And did we mention that you'd receive special prices if you choose to be a Member or an IBO? That's right, good prices plus good service, all from the comfort and convenience of your own home.

Don't worry about quality either. The guarantees you'll find at the Quixtar site will be better than just about anywhere you're shopping now. So what are you waiting for? Let's **Go Shopping!**

THE SEVEN TYPES OF SHOPPERS

Each one of us likes to approach shopping a little differently. Some of us could while away a whole day at the mall with no trouble at all. Others hate to shop and want to make shopping as quick and painless as possible. We've taken an informal survey of our friends and found that there are basically seven types of shoppers. And the Quixtar site offers a shopping experience that's the perfect match for each one.

Take a look at the list below and identify your shopping personality. Then, turn to the section in this guidebook that describes the steps you'll take to shop the way you want to shop – click-by-click™.

1. The Get-Me-Out-Of-Here-Quick Shopper - You're a busy person. You know what you want. Stock numbers. Case lots. Literature and business support materials. You want a **Quick Order** experience. In. And out.

Click on the View Cart icon on any page and go directly to your shopping cart. To **Add an item to my cart**, enter the **Qty** and **SKU** in the boxes provided and click Add To Cart. Large orders are faster if you click on Multi-Line Form and go to it. Click Check Out, in the red box, when you're done.

2. The I-Need-A-Personal-Shopping-Assistant Shopper - You're balancing your roles as best you can – family, job, friends, activities. You want to keep up with the current trends but you don't have time to look through everything yourself. You want someone to bring you just the stuff you're looking for and then let you choose what you want to buy.

    *Click in the **Search** box in the navy blue navigational bar at the top of your screen. Type in what you're looking for. You could type a word or two, like **tank top** or **swimsuit**. Or you could type a stock number you've used before, like **WE1**. Click GO! and you'll get a list of items to choose from that match your criteria. Click on the description to see more details, including pictures. Then click Add to drop it in your cart.*

3. The Find-The-Shopping-Directory Shopper - You're the shopper who goes into a new mall and heads straight for the illuminated shopping directory to see which stores are where. You locate the big "You are Here" X, get your bearings, find your targets, and go!

    *Start at the Home Page where you log in. You'll see a **Shopping Directory** with categories like Health, Beauty, Home Care, Housewares, Pets, Food, Baby, Office, Electronics, Services, Fashion, Gardening, Personal Products, Gifts, Leisure, Toys, Sports and Automotive. Click on the category you want and you'll see a list of shops to choose from. Click on the shop you want and you'll go right to it.*

4. The Go-Right-To-My-Favorite-Stores Shopper - You've got certain stores that you know will have all your favorite stuff. No wonder you always head for those places first.

*Start at the Home Page where you log in. Click on
Alphabetical Listing shown in red at the top of your
screen. You'll see stores listed by name in alphabetical
order. Look over the list until you find your favorite, then
click on the name of the store and go!*

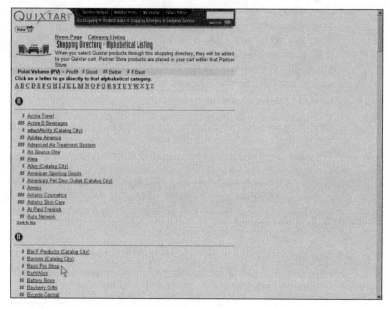

FIGURE 4-1 ALPHABETICAL INDEX

5. The Go-Right-To-My-Favorite-Product Shopper - You've
    got certain products that you simply can't live without.
    You're not sure which stores will carry them. But you
    know exactly which products you want.

    *Start at the Home Page where you log in. Click on
    Product Index shown in red at the top of your screen.
    You'll see products listed by name in alphabetical order.
    Look over the list until you find your favorite, then click on
    the name of the product and go!*

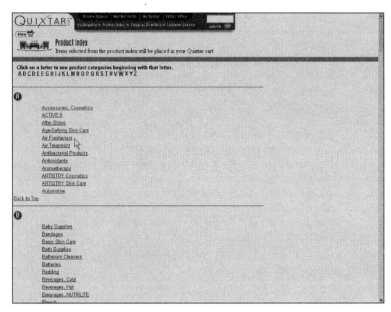

FIGURE 4-2 PRODUCT INDEX

6.   The Shop-'Til-You-Drop Shopper - You've managed to
     elevate shopping to an art form. A full day of shopping
     for most people would be exhausting, but for you it's just
     the beginning! You're rarely in a hurry when you shop.
     Browsing through all the choices you see is half the fun!

     Click on Go Shopping *in the navy blue navigational bar on
     any page. Then, wander around the site, clicking on
     whatever catches your attention. If you're looking for
     variety, visit the* Partner Stores *and spend some time in
     Catalog City. If value is more your style, be sure to look
     around* My Home, My Health, My Self, Hot Buys *and the
     Store For More. Click on anything that looks interesting
     whether it's a picture or a description of something you
     like. If you want to hold an item while you think it over,
     just click on* Add To Cart. *You don't have to pay for
     anything until you go through the* Check Out.

7. The Give-It-To-Me-One-More-Time Shopper - Once you've found the products that work for you, you'd be so much happier if you didn't have to keep going out to get them time and time again. After all, you don't have to call your local electric company to keep the power coming month after month. So why should you have to keep going out to the store to get the same things over and over again?

Start at the Home Page where you log in. Click on Hotspots on the left side of your screen and select Ditto Delivery. You'll be able to set up a profile that keeps your favorite products coming to you automatically for as long as you like. You'll choose the products you want and specify the delivery schedule. Isn't that a relief? See Click 16 Product Ordering for more details on Ditto Delivery.

SHOPPING CARTS

Since shopping at Quixtar is a little like shopping at a mall, you'll use different shopping carts and separate checkouts for certain kinds of purchases. You can shop in all of the Quixtar stores – **My Home**, **My Health**, **My Self**, **Store For More**, and **Hot Buys** – using just one shopping cart and one checkout.

Anytime you want to see what's in your Quixtar shopping cart, look up at the top left of the your screen. You'll see a little shopping cart icon. Just click on View to see what's in your basket. You can also add or delete items from your basket quickly by using this shortcut.

Icon A small picture, usually a symbol, that you can click on with your mouse in order to do something. Quixtar icons can link you to another page on the site, add an item to your cart, and more. Icons, sometimes called buttons, are like picture shortcuts to help you perform repetitive tasks.

FIGURE 4-3   GO SHOPPING FRONT PAGE

Look up at the top of your screen in the navy blue navigational bar and click on Go Shopping. Now, next to the shopping cart icon, you'll see **My Home**, **My Health**, **My Self**, **Hot Buys**, **Store For More**, and **Partner Stores**. See the icon to the left of the **Partner Stores**? It looks like a little globe with an arrow through it. That's there to remind you that you are headed to completely separate stores that partner with Quixtar to bring you a wider range of products and great deals. Partner Stores have their own easy-to-use shopping carts and checkouts.

Will You Keep an Eye on My Cart, Please?
When you've added items to your shopping cart, you'll notice that a red object appears in the basket of the shopping cart icon. If you don't want to checkout yet, those items will still be in your cart, ready and waiting for you, when you come back. Try that at your local store!

QUIXTAR EXCLUSIVES

Begin your shopping experience with the **Quixtar Exclusives**. These items, found in the **My Home**, **My Health**, and **My Self** sections of the site, offer the best values on things you routinely need.

My Home includes products for Laundry, Cleaners & Disinfectants, Water Treatment, Cookware & Cutlery, Tableware, Crystal and Giftware, and Home Services.

My Health includes Vitamins, Performance Foods, Therapeutic Magnets, Weight Management and other items to improve your health.

My Self includes products for Hair Care, Skin Care, a Cosmetics Counter and Aromatherapy.

Many of these items you purchase month after month, so it's a real bonus that they are such excellent values. You can even set these items up on a pre-arranged delivery schedule, called **Ditto Delivery**ˢᴹ, so that they arrive at your door automatically, whenever you request them.

HOT BUYS

Here you'll find the best prices on all kinds of stuff. A recent visit to **Hot Buys** found dozens of items, including a Seiko® Men's Watch, regularly priced at $150.00, for $49.99, and a Bill Blass® Club Bag, for weekend travel, regularly priced at $39.99, for only $9.99.

STORE FOR MORE

Select from hundreds of items by name-brand manufacturers, at spectacular prices, all under one roof. The **SFM** has departments just like the large stores you're used to shopping in. A sampling of items found in a recent visit to the **Store For More** (and the department we found them in), included a ladies silk and cashmere sweater for $39.99 (**Fashion**), Arizona® Green Tea with Ginseng and Honey, $23.99 for 24 drink boxes (**Convenience**), a Sharp® Compact Plain Paper Fax Machine for $109.99, after manufacturer's rebate (**Electronics**), a Cuisinart® 10-cup Coffeemaker and Coffee Grinder for $79.99 (**Home**), a Curve® by Liz Claiborne fragrance gift set for women for $80, a $148 value (**Holiday**), and a Bell South 25-Channel Cordless Phone with Digital Answering Machine for $39.99 (**Hot Buys**).

PARTNER STORES

Connect to a multitude of quality online shopping sites that will provide you with thousands of products and services. You won't believe the vast selection of choices available to you through the Partner Store sites! And the best news of all is that Members earn Q-Credits and IBOs get PV for each item purchased from a Partner Store that they visit through Quixtar.

 Get More Bang for Your Buck Attention IBOs: Items purchased from the Quixtar Exclusive Stores will give you more PV per dollar spent than items purchased anywhere else. Shop here first & watch your PV multiply fast!

CLICK 5   MY HOME

CLICK HERE TO ENRICH THE HOURS YOU SPEND AT HOME. YOU'LL FIND WAYS TO MAKE YOUR TIME AT HOME MORE PRODUCTIVE & MORE ENJOYABLE. EVERY HOME REQUIRES HOUSEWORK TO MAINTAIN IT. IN THIS SECTION YOU'LL DISCOVER PRODUCTS, SOLUTIONS & TIPS TO EASE YOUR LOAD & CREATE MORE TIME TO SPEND WITH YOUR FAMILY & FRIENDS – AT HOME, OF COURSE.

MY HOME

WHAT'S NEW

Don't you just love making improvements around your home? Those special touches that make a house a home, inside and out. Each time we enter **My Home** at Quixtar, we always look around this section first. There's always something different, something better. Get the scoop on the newest features and products for your home. You'll see them here first.

Each week there are new recipes in the **Cooking Club** section. Make your menu planning a bit easier by trying out these fresh, seasonal suggestions.

SPECIAL OFFERS

Check out the **Special Offers**. There may be anywhere from a few, to a few dozen, items on special each time you visit. We especially liked the College Survival Kit we recently found in this section. It included a Sports Drink, Echinacea, and a clever laundry idea that combines detergent and fabric softener in one handy pouch that goes from washer to dryer. All specially discounted for college budgets.

Click Now or Forever Hold Your Mouse
Special offers change frequently so if you see something that looks like a good deal – it is! Click it into your shopping basket now to avoid the disappointment you'll feel when you return to snap up that deal later on, only to find that it went "poof" while you were thinking about it.

EXPERT ADVICE

Everyone can give advice about something. Just ask your co-worker, or the person in line behind you at the deli counter. Whatever you want to know, they've got an opinion and they'll be glad to share it with you. But expert advice, now that's something altogether different. If you want a qualified opinion, it'll usually cost you plenty. But not at Quixtar.

Let's say you have a question about the safety of your drinking water. There's an expert right there, on your screen. Yep, he's got degrees in Biology and Chemistry, plus a Masters in Biochemistry and a Ph.D. in Chemistry. Previously in research for the FDA, Dr. Roy Kuennen holds three patents for water treatment systems design and has published over 30 articles in technical journals. That's an expert all right! And there he is with an answer to your question, which just happens to be the **Question of the Day**.

Question – Is chlorine in my drinking water good or bad?
Answer – Treating water with chlorine is good. Unfortunately, drinking it can be bad. Then he gives you all the reasons why. In plain English.

You can also look at **FAQs** on this subject or **Visit our Archive** for past expert columns and Q&A.

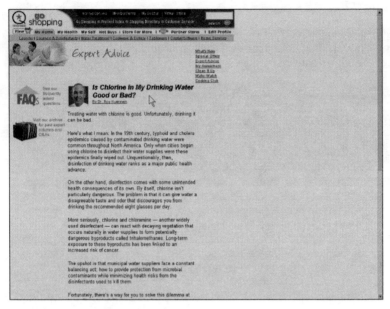

FIGURE 5-1   EXPERT ADVICE

MY ASSESSMENT

This is cool. Remember taking quizzes in school where there was only one right answer to every question? Not here. The right answer is *your* answer. This time. And every time. Even if your answer changes. It's still right.

This is how it works. You'll breeze through these multiple-choice questions about your laundry, the type of stains you get, your drinking water, your cleaning challenges, your cooking style, etc. Then, you'll click a button and voila, you'll receive a personalized assessment based on all of your responses. Right in front of you will be product suggestions to complement your lifestyle and solve your specific challenges. If you like what you see, and we're sure you will, one more click will drop items into your shopping cart and you're on your way. Now that's cool, wouldn't you agree?

CLEAN IT UP

Architects, builders and designers take note. It's time to roll out the blueprints here. This section gives you a **Housecleaning Blueprint**, which takes you through the kitchen, to the bathroom, the living area, and finally to the bedroom of your house. In each room, you'll find strategies for bringing out the best, and cleanest, your home has to offer. Just click on the room you need help with and you'll be greeted with step-by-step instructions for conquering your toughest tasks. The products you need to assist you will be highlighted here for you and with a click of your mouse you can drop them into your shopping cart. Now you're one step closer to a home that sparkles and shines!

Stains don't stand a chance now that you have the secrets to getting rid of them. Click on **Stain Remedies** and embark on an interactive adventure to eliminate even your most stubborn stains. You'll identify the type of stain you need removed - grease, lipstick, coffee, blood, grass, and mud are just a few of over 50 you have to choose from. Next, click on the blue Stain Remedy button at the bottom of your screen. Then, watch the stain wizard whip up a remedy for even your worst stain nightmares. You'll see remedies for all kinds of stained items – laundry, carpet, hard surfaces and more. Once you know the secret, you can click on the products you need and drop them into your shopping basket. And move on to more important things – like where are you going to wear that expensive dress that you've just saved from the spot monster?

Just What the Doctor Ordered If your home is anything like ours, piles of dirty laundry just appear overnight. It's enough to make you feel like throwing in the towel. How would you like a **Laundry Prescription** to come to your rescue? Just answer a few questions and you'll receive a customized solution to your laundry woes. Drop these wonderful products into your shopping cart with the click of a mouse & you'll be on the road to recovery in no time.

If you or someone in your family suffers from asthma or allergies, you'll want to check out **Healthy Tips for My Home.** Here you'll find sensible suggestions for getting rid of airborne allergens created by dust mites, pet dander, mold, and even cockroaches.

WATER WATCH

Eight glasses a day. We know we're supposed to drink eight glasses a day of good, clean water for optimal health. Whether you measure up to the recommended amount or not, you'll want to make sure that the water you do drink is clean and safe. **Water Watch** gives you links to organizations that study water day in and day out. See what the Environmental Protection Agency has to say about water quality in your part of the country. Get information about NSF Certified products for drinking water. Read reports about the health effects of drinking water contaminants like lead, chlorine, and parasites. Find a water treatment system that protects your family. It's all here, at **Water Watch**.

COOKING CLUB

Stop in at the **Cooking Club** for a look at this week's **Recipes**. Each menu is designed by the Chef of the Month. We visited during football season and found wonderful recipes for a Tailgater Party by Chef Karin Orr, a food writer and PBS cooking show host. Whether you go out to the game, or watch it from home, you'll enjoy these recipes for Handwarmer Tomato Soup, Cheesy Buns, Lemon Chicken on a Stick, Crunchy Broccoli Salad and Tasty Apple Turnovers.

You'll also find **Cooking Tips**. Those little tricks your grandmother knew are here along with some tips from today's professional restaurant kitchens. Bon Appetit!

GO SHOPPING

Everything you need for taking care of your home is at your fingertips in the **My Home** section of **Go Shopping**. You'll find all the products you need grouped together in sections like **Laundry, Cleaners and Disinfectants, Water Treatment, Cookware and Cutlery, Tableware,** and **Crystal and Giftware**. Just click on the group you need and you'll find all the **Quixtar Exclusives** for that group listed on the left side of your screen.

FIGURE 5-2   MY HOME

Pick an item from the list, and click on it to see pictures of all the products that fit that description, along with a short description of each item and your price. Once you've found what you want, click on Add to drop it into your shopping cart. Or, you can zoom in on one specific item by clicking on its picture to expand it to a full page. Now you'll see a little more about the item's features and benefits. You'll still have the Add button there for when you're ready to click it. If you want More Info, like ingredients or suggested use instructions, there's a button to click for that, too.

It's Never Over 'til It's Over   Don't worry about adding things to your basket. You can change your mind & take them out later, before you complete the checkout process. Or, you can change the quantity if you decide you want more or less or something.

Watch for **You May Also Like** on the right side of your screen. This area features items that are frequently selected by people who buy what you are looking at. You'll see a few pictures here that may interest you. To jump to one of these other items, just click on the picture or the name of the item. You can always go back to where you were by using the Back button on your Browser.

Is This Your Best Price?   No, this isn't a cyber-flea market, but chances are you can get a better price. For better pricing, Clients can register as Members. And Members can register as IBOs. IBOs get the best prices plus they can boost their income potential by referring more people to the site & increasing their volume. Get it? Got it? Good!

Honey, Have You Seen the Toothpaste?   If you can't find something, try typing its name in the white search box found in the navy blue bar at the top of the page. Rather than typing in a certain brand name, it's better to search for "toothpaste". If you know the Quixtar stock number, you can type it in the search box instead. Then click **Go** and it will appear!

SHOPPING CART

Each time you click something into your shopping cart, you'll be taken to the **Shopping Cart** page. Wouldn't it be great if you could see a running total of the stuff you've placed in your cart before you go through the checkout line? So you could make any changes before they collect your money? Well, with Quixtar you can! If you want to take something out of your cart, just click the Delete button next to that item. Your order will reflect this change automatically. Or change a quantity by clicking on the Qty shown and replacing it with a different number. Then click the Update Cart button to see the changes in your order.

Along the top of the **Shopping Cart** screen, you'll see a narrow
navy blue bar with some features you'll find useful – **Check Out**,
Return to Shopping, and **Ordering Help**. Click on any one of
these and they'll take you exactly where they say. Ordering Help
takes you to a screen that will answer any questions you may
have about completing your order. Check Out takes you to the
next screen in the checkout process. And if you want to keep the
stuff that's in your cart, but don't want to pay for it yet, just click
Return to Shopping and it will all still be there whenever you're
ready for it.

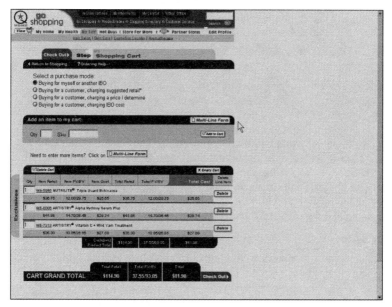

FIGURE 5-3 QUIXTAR SHOPPING CART

If you are an IBO, you will see a few pricing options listed just
above your order. If you are not **Buying for myself or another
IBO**, you can select from **charging suggested retail, charging
IBO cost**, or **charging a price I determine**. Select the one you
want by clicking in the little circle. The pricing will update
automatically when you click in the circle you want. When you're

ready to checkout, click Check Out, found in the red bar, at the top or at the bottom of your screen.

Two, Two, Two Carts in One   If your order includes items from Quixtar Exclusives – My Home, My Health, My Self and Hot Buys – and items from the Store For More, you'll see separate totals on your Shopping Cart page. Never fear, you'll only have to go through one checkout. Since your orders will ship from two different warehouses, you'll see separate shipping options. And you'll get two separate invoice numbers. But only one checkout!

The next screen will ask you to verify your **Shipping Information**. It's already set to **My Shipping Address**.   You'll see your address in a beige bar so you can verify its accuracy. IBOs will also have the option of **Ship to Another IBO**. Click in that circle if you want the order sent to another IBO. Then fill in **Their IBO #** in the box provided and their address will be filled in automatically. You may also choose to **Specify Shipping Address** if you'd like to send the order elsewhere. To do this, click in the circle and then type in the **Name, Address**, and **Phone Number** information requested.

Now, click on Check Out, in the red bar, to move to the **Shipping Options** screen. Here you'll select your desired shipping option by clicking in the circle next to the delivery method you prefer. Choose from Premium Next Day, Premium Second Day, Ground Express (3-5 business day delivery) and Standard (cycle), which will arrive in 3-10 business days. Click Check Out.

Now you are at the **Order Preview** screen. Your entire order will be displayed, line-by-line, for your approval. You'll also see the tax and shipping charges and your totals. Your email address will also be shown since you'll receive an email confirmation when this order is placed.

Payment Information can now be entered. Click in the circle to select your preferred method of payment, either **Credit Card** or **Bank Draft**. For Credit Card, type in the **Name**, exactly as it appears on the credit card. Select the Card Type and Expiration Date by clicking on the arrow in the drop-down boxes. Fill in the box with your **Card Number**. Type in the number without dashes and without spaces.   If you select **Bank Draft**, type in your **PIN Number** in the box provided.

IBOs who want **Volume to Follow** the order can enter the **IBO's Last Name** and **IBO's Number** here. Then, when everything is just the way you want it, click on the red Purchase button.

Congratulations! You've successfully entered your online order. Isn't this exciting? The next screen you'll see will be your **Order Confirmation**. Your **Invoice Number** will be shown in red under **Order Details**.

Get into the Express Lane   If you want to get to the front of the checkout line from anywhere in the site, just click on the **View Cart** shopping basket icon located to the left of the navy blue navigational bar at the top of your screen. Remember, Partner Stores have separate checkouts.

Don't Touch that Dial   Oops, even with all the chances you had to make changes, you've accidentally finalized your order & you made a mistake. Relax! Click on **Customer Service, About My Order, View Order History,** & then click the **Invoice #**. When you see the order detail, click **Cancel this Order**. Now you're back to the Order History screen and that Invoice # is marked as **Cancelled**. If you change your mind again, click on the Invoice #, then click **Place This Order Again**. You'll get a new Invoice # this time around. Just be sure you do all this flip-flopping before the scheduled ship date!

HOME SERVICES

Family is the true heart of any home. **Home Services** help you stay in touch, watch over the people you hold dear, and provide you with the tools to balance your roles and focus on what matters most. IBOs earn PV on the use of most of these services. Click on **First Alert** for professional security systems, **MCI WorldCom** for long distance phone calling, **FranklinCovey** for time management tools, **QuixNet** for family-friendly Internet Service, **Realty & Mortgage Services**, or **Universal Insurance Services** for your medical, dental, life, disability, auto, and home insurance needs.

CLICK 6 MY HEALTH

CLICK HERE TO FIND VITAMINS, NUTRITIONAL SUPPLEMENTS, & HERBALS TO SUPPORT YOUR HEALTHY LIFESTYLE. AND INFORMATION YOU CAN TRUST FROM LEADING MEDICAL EXPERTS. YOU'LL ALSO FIND PERFORMANCE FOODS, THERAPEUTIC MAGNETS & A HIGH-TECH, HIGH-TOUCH WEIGHT MANAGEMENT PROGRAM. ALL FROM THE COMPANY THAT CARES ABOUT YOU.

MY HEALTH

WHAT'S NEW

Gone are the days when simple advice like "an apple a day keeps the doctor away" was all we needed to know about health and nutrition. With today's hectic lifestyles, "early to bed and early to rise" often becomes late to bed and early to rise. Throw in families with two working parents, or single-parent households and we've really got our hands full. Taking care of the necessities means we sometimes forget to take care of ourselves. This part of the site is just for you. Spend just a few minutes a day here and you will leave armed with information and strategies to improve your health. And if you feel better, you'll be better equipped to handle whatever life sends your way.

A click on What's New will introduce you to the latest and greatest products to enhance your healthy lifestyle. You'll find items backed by scientific research and clinical experience. Nutritional supplements designed to support your specific needs. Links to sites for medical organizations that have the facts you're looking for. Expert advice. Products with integrity. Credible information from a source you can trust. It's all here at **My Health**.

FIGURE 6-1   MY HEALTH

SPECIAL OFFERS

Here you'll find special pricing on some of your favorite nutrition and wellness products. These specials don't last long, so stop by everyday and take advantage of discounts on things you use every month. There may be anywhere from a few, to a few dozen, items on special each time you visit. We especially liked the "Baby It's Cold Outside and That's Where it Should Stay" – a combo of Echinacea, Vitamin C, Garlic with Licorice, and Vitamin A with Zinc. This quartet of specially selected supplements will fortify you when the days turn cold outside. And your wallet will appreciate the substantial savings.

EXPERT ADVICE

So you've got pain. Most everybody does. But you're not sure if it's worth booking a doctor's appointment. Or maybe you've already been to the doctor and you've still got pain. If only there was an expert on pain you could consult. You would. You really should. And you can. Right here, at your fingertips, in **My Health**.

Dr. Robert Holcomb is an expert all right. He's got an M.D., a Ph. D., holds multiple patents, and is a Diplomat in the American Academy of Pain Management. Now that's an expert! He's written a column on pain and he's designed some effective new therapies for reducing pain. Your pain. Isn't it great to have an expert around?

You can also look at **FAQs** on this subject or **Visit our Archive** for past expert columns.

MY ASSESSMENT

Whenever we go to a new doctor, they always ask us to fill out a long questionnaire about our medical history. **My Assessment** is somewhat like that. But it includes lifestyle questions as well as medical history questions. Questions about your diet, your stress level, your energy level, your memory, and how well you sleep. Questions about the health of your joints, your liver, your heart, and more. When you click off your answers to these multiple-choice questions, click on Submit, and you'll receive a customized assessment based on all of your responses. Right in front of you will be product suggestions to enhance your lifestyle and address your specific needs. Click on any product you want to know more about. If you like what you see, one more click on Add will drop items into your shopping cart and you'll be on your way to a healthier tomorrow.

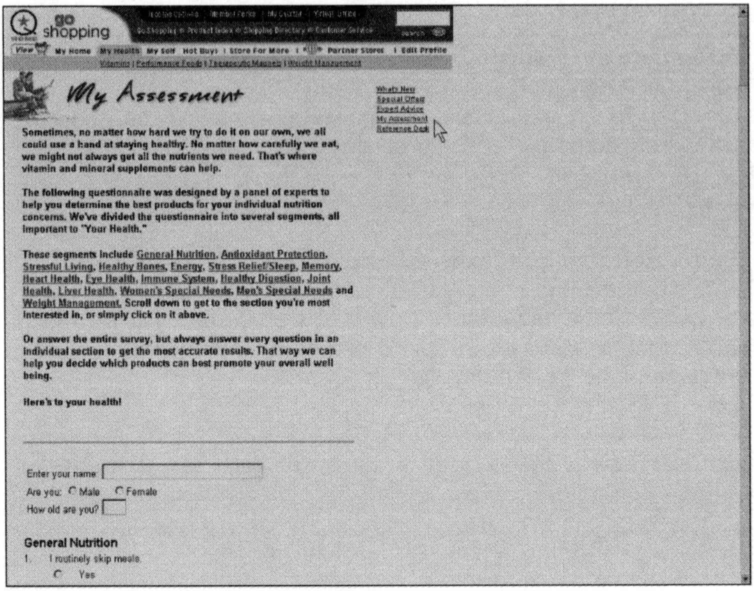

FIGURE 6-2   MY ASSESSMENT

REFERENCE DESK

If you're like us, you sometimes need a little help interpreting the medical information your doctor gives you. Or perhaps you want a second opinion. The **Reference Desk** contains a number of wonderful research tools to provide you with the answers you're looking for. This part of the site provides a very valuable service. It's saved us several trips to the pediatrician already.

Use **InfoFinder** to search the databases for current information on whatever issue you need to know more about. Just type a **keyword or phrase** in the search box and click Find. You'll be able choose from a list of articles on your topic. A search on **pregnancy** found general articles on pregnancy as well as articles on weight gain, nutrition for pregnant and lactating women, herbals useful during pregnancy and amino-acid production. Also listed are recommended Nutrilite® products that may provide nutritional support for the condition you researched. In this case, Nutrilite® Iron-Folic Plus was suggested during pregnancy. Click on the product link and you'll jump to a page that gives detailed product information and lets you Add it to your shopping cart.

Today's Health News is a service provided by Johns Hopkins Health Information. Here you'll find articles on Today in Health History, a Health Tip of the Day, This Week in Health, Ask-the-Doc, Pollen and Pollution Forecasts for 50 Cities, and more.

If you have questions on common **Diseases and Conditions**, you'll find answers here that are easy to understand. There's a section **For Health Professionals** that links to **TopicDoc**, a topic driven clinical literature service. Online **Physician Referrals** are also available at the **Reference Desk** using the AMA Physician Referral service.

GO SHOPPING

If your get up and go just got up and went, this section can help you get it back. You've already taken a step toward reducing the stress in your life by deciding to shop online – instead of in line. And less stress means better health. But there's more. How's your diet?

We all know we should eat lots of nutrient-rich foods, like fruit, vegetables, low-fat dairy products, and whole grains. But if you're like us, you often don't have the time to ensure your meals are balanced and nutritionally complete. You'll feel a lot better if you add a good multivitamin and mineral supplement to your daily routine.

One click on Vitamins will lead you to some of the best supplements available today. Here you'll find solutions for everyone in the family. **Chewables** for children, **Liquid Vitamins** for babies, and **Antioxidants** for grown-ups. **Herbals** you'll reach for time and again, like Echinacea, Ginseng with Gingko, and St. John's Wort. Plus **Other Supplements** you rely on like Calcium, Omega3, and Glucosamine. If the vitamin maze is still too confusing to you, spend a few minutes taking **My Assessment** and the clouds will begin to clear. Your body will thank you.

Click on Performance Foods to find energy bars and sports drinks for your next workout or the kid's soccer team.

Remember when a kiss from your mother was all it took to ease the pain and make your boo-boo better? It's good to know that relief is still available even if mother is not. Click on Therapeutic Magnets to discover an amazing technology to help you block the pain when it hurts. These **Quixtar℠ Exclusives** are the only magnets used at the Center for Pain Research. Top quality, not cheap imitations. Experience the difference. Relief can be just a click away!

Have you ever wondered why eating a two-pound box of chocolates can show up as five pounds on your bathroom scale? Or why some people can eat gallons of ice cream and not put on a single ounce while you gain weight just walking by your favorite bakery? **Weight Management** is not a simple proposition. If it were, we'd all be walking around in the body of our choice. But there is hope. Join the Fit Crew and learn how you can lose pounds, not your lifestyle.

 **Set Yourself Up for Success** It's a fact. Seventy percent of dieters who go it alone fail. So join the Fit Crew. You'll get one-to-one help where you want it, how you want it, and when you need it. Go ahead, step up to success!

You'll never be alone with this program. You'll have access to online support groups to discuss the plan, the products, exercise, recipes and meal plans. They'll share your frustrations and celebrate your successes. Or you can talk to a personal coach over the phone if you prefer. Either way, when you join this team, you'll have the products and support you need to give you the advantage you've been looking for. The **Trim Advantage™**.

CLICK 7   MY SELF

CLICK HERE TO ENTER A PRIVATE WORLD THAT REVOLVES AROUND YOU. YOUR SKIN. YOUR HAIR. YOUR FACE. SEE WHAT'S HOT THIS SEASON. TRY MAKE-UP ON ONLINE WITH VIRTUAL LOOK. CREATE A LOOK THAT'S YOURS AND YOURS ALONE. A TEAM OF EXPERTS IS STANDING BY TO ASSIST YOU. BUT THE DECISION IS YOURS, AND YOURS ALONE. AFTER ALL, THERE WILL NEVER BE ANOTHER YOU.

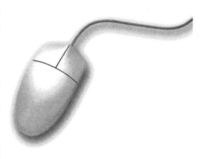

MY SELF

WHAT'S NEW

Long, long ago, in a land far away, the only lady in the land who had a beauty consultant was the queen. And even she couldn't always get a straight answer from that mirror on the wall. You, on the other hand, have not one – but an entire staff of advisors - at your beck and call in the **My Self** section of the site.

You'll fall in love with this way of shopping for your cosmetics, skin and hair care products. You'll find the best quality products, along with lots of tips to keep your look fresh and exciting. All without the high pressure you might be accustomed to feeling at the cosmetics counter of your local department store. What a beautiful feeling!

Make sure you stop by **What's New** every time you visit this part of the site. If you do, you'll be the first to know about the latest shades for the coming season. You'll get tips from the pros. See how to update your look, step-by-step. Discover new anti-aging products. Find ways to pamper yourself. All from the privacy of your own home. You're going to love it here!

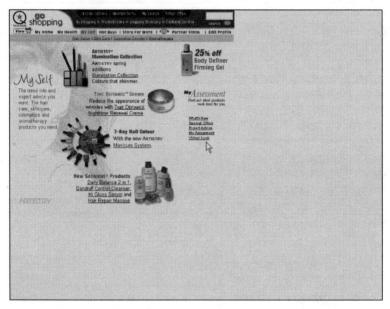

FIGURE 7-1   MY SELF

SPECIAL OFFERS

While you're here, take a look at the **Special Offers**. There may be anywhere from a few, to a few dozen, items on special each time you visit. We especially liked the Aromatherapy Systems we found during a recent visit. Each system included a body mist, bath and shower gel, body bar and body lotion. In your choice of four fabulous blends – calming, energizing, balancing or enticing. Created from all-natural essential oils and specially priced to pamper your pocketbook while they pamper you!

Expert Advice

Your schedule is, well, shall we say, "challenging"? When you leave home in the morning, the hours seem to fly by and before you know it, the sun has set and yet you're still going. To school. Ballet. Little League. PTA. A quick dinner. An evening business appointment. And so it goes. And so you go.

It's good to know that there is someone out there who understands. Who knows you're busy. Involved. Committed. But still want to look your best, from morning to night.

You'll find real life **Expert Advice** here, from real experts. Like Coreen Cordova. She's a nationally recognized beauty expert with decades of creative experience in the cosmetics industry. She understands what it's like. That's why she wrote a column titled "Desk to Dinner: Looking Your Best from Office Desk to Dance Floor". It's packed full of tips to carry you through your day in style.

You'll also want to read the **Question of the Day**. Each one is answered by an expert. You'll pick up pointers here on hair, make-up and skin care.

For more tricks from the pros you can also search the **FAQs** by topic or **Visit our Archive** for past expert columns.

My Assessment

Celebrities have long enjoyed the benefits of knowing how to showcase their best features and draw attention away from their physical flaws. Now you, too, can share their secrets by finding the beauty products that bring out the best in you. Just answer the questions on **My Assessment** and you'll receive a customized personal plan that will let you arrive with confidence, wherever you go. You'll find questions on your hair, your skin, and your natural coloring.

When you click off your answers to these multiple-choice questions, click on Submit, and you'll receive a customized assessment based on all of your responses. You'll see product recommendations to pamper your hair and scalp, bring out your glowing complexion, match your skin to flattering foundation shades, and show you the cosmetic colors that are just right for you. No guessing. No mistakes. No pressure. Now that you have all the right answers, one more click on Add will drop these must-have goodies into your shopping cart.

Click With Confidence   Unlike the products you used to buy at the mall or from your hair stylist, these **Quixtar Exclusives** are backed by a satisfaction guarantee. So if a color looks different on you than it did when you were shopping – relax – you don't have to live with anything that doesn't work out for you.

VIRTUAL LOOK

Remember when you were growing up? How you used to sneak into your mother's closet and step into her high-heeled shoes. You'd try on her hats, scarves and jewelry until you found that look that was uniquely you. And then came the toughest decision. Which lipstick to use? Pink perhaps, or red. No, coral – that's the one! Oh, look at that one – it's frosted! That would be better yet. By the time you'd tried them all, you were a sight to behold.

Recapture the fun of experimenting with color, without the mess, with **Virtual Look**.

Virtual   Short for virtual reality, and sometimes called VR, virtual refers to computer simulations of real-world activities that use 3-D graphics to allow you to interact with the simulation. You will move through a virtual experience as though you were participating in it in real life.

You'll need to download a small file in order to experience **Virtual Look**. Don't worry, this will only take a minute. Click on Virtual Look, then click the blue Continue button and the file will download all by itself. You won't have to hunt down the file

anywhere. Your screen will just go right into showing you the
Virtual Look face.

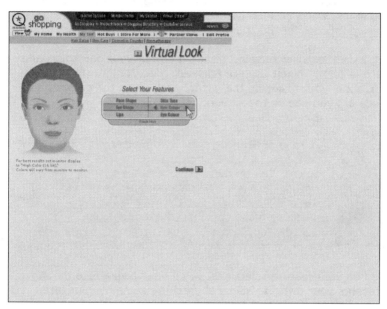

FIGURE 7-2   VIRTUAL LOOK

Download   Downloading is a way you can use
your modem to "pull down" software or other
files that belong to another computer and use
them like they were your own. But the original
owner can still use the file, too. It's sort of like
a teenage child "downloading" money from
their parents' wallets to their own. Unlike the
files, though, chances are the parents will never
get to use that money again.

First, you'll select your features. Click on the little arrow to choose
the shape of your face, your eyes and your lips. When you are
choosing a feature, the text for that feature will change from blue

to red and you'll see two red arrows next to the red text. Click on these arrows to change the feature type until you get just the one you want. You'll choose the shape of your face from oval, round, square or rectangular, diamond or heart-shaped. When you have the one you want, click on the next feature and repeat the selection process for the shape of your eyes and your lips.

Next, click the arrow to select your skin tone, your hair color, and your eye color. When you are finished, click Continue to move on. Then, apply your make-up the virtual way, using the brushes and applicators you see on the screen.

You're a Shining Star   No matter who you are, you'll enjoy using these cosmetics from one of the top five cosmetic brands in the world. And you'll be delighted at the prices. IBOs will be smiling all the way to the bank because these cosmetics have high point values, too.

Based on your feature selections, you'll be shown a face that represents your own. It will be shaped the same as your face. It will have the same hair, eye, and skin color. Now the fun begins! At the bottom of your screen, you'll see a row of make-up brushes and applicators. Click on the first one, that's the blush brush. You'll notice just above the brush, several blush colours have appeared. These are the colours that are recommended for you based on the selections you made earlier. They are grouped into cool, warm or neutral shades for your convenience. You'll also see their name and price.

Click on the colour of your choice and watch as it appears on your **Virtual Face**. You'll even see a customized make-up application tip based on the face you've created. Oval faces, for example, will find that their blush should be applied just under the cheekbone and blended toward the top of the ear.

Now that you see how that colour will look on your face, you can click on Add to List and go on with your make-up session. You don't need to stop and write anything down, all that is taken care of for you. These items will be added to a temporary shopping list for you. Later, if you decide to purchase them, you will able to add them to your shopping cart. Click on the question button or the back arrow, located at the top of your screen next to the Virtual Look sign, if you want to go back a page or get more information on how Virtual Look works.

Continue creating your **Virtual Look** by clicking on the eye pencil, then the eye shadow applicator, the lip pencil, and lastly, the lipstick. Each click will bring up the colours chosen especially for you. Play a little. Try different colors. Anything you like you can place on your list.

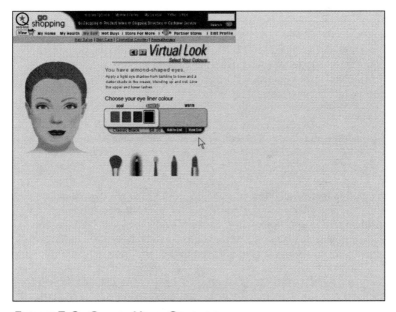

FIGURE 7-3 SELECT YOUR COLOURS

When you're done, click View List. The colours you have selected will be listed for you to consider. Now is the time to decide what you want. If you see something on **Your Shopping List** that you want to delete, just highlight the quantity with a click of your mouse and change it to **0**. You can also order multiples of the

same item by increasing the quantity. Click Add to Cart and you
will on your way to the checkout.

GO SHOPPING

Ladies, this may well become your favorite part of the entire site.
Because it's all about you. **My Self** gives you everything you need
to put your best face forward. Let's start in the **Hair Salon**. Click
on What's Hot in Hair. Here you'll find photos of great new hair
looks for the upcoming season. If you see one you might like to
try, click on How to Create this Look.

You'll get step-by-step instructions on how to achieve this fantastic
style. These are the same styles that would set you back plenty if
you went to your hairdresser. Instead, stay home, relax, and let
internationally renowned master hair stylist, John Gillespie, guide
you each step of the way. He'll tell you which products to use to
get that fabulous look. And if you need one of the products he
recommends, just click on Add and it will drop right into your
shopping cart. Now, wasn't that fun?

If you'd like some more tips from the pros, click on Hair 101.
You'll find secrets here on **Hair Care** and **Hair Styling**. Just one
of these tidbits made such a difference in our hair. We couldn't
believe we'd never heard this technique before. Okay, okay, here
it is: If you use conditioner all over your hair, it will weigh hair
down at the roots, making it look dull and limp. Apply your
conditioner only where your hair needs it – from the middle
lengths to the ends, not on the roots. You'll find out how to get
great volume and body, how to create the texture you want, and
the best way to use your blow dryer to get the look you want.

You'll find all the products you need to keep your tresses in top
shape in the **Hair Salon**. **Shampoos**, **Conditioners**, **Treatment
Products**, and **Styling Products**. And they're all salon quality.
Just click your way to the most beautiful head of hair you've ever
had!

Next, let's take a look at **Skin Care**. Even the best make-up
around can't cover up skin that hasn't been cared for. Choose a
Basic Skin Care system and stick with it. You know the basics –
cleanse, tone, and moisturize. There are systems here for every

skin type – normal, dry, oily, or sensitive. Only the best natural ingredients go into these essential items. Once you have your basics covered, take a look at the **Special Treatment** and **Age-Defying Skin Care** products. You'll find cutting-edge products with ingredients like Alpha Hydroxy. And Vitamin C. Incredible anti-aging products that will make your skin look and feel better.

While you're here, click on What's Hot in Skin Care to see the latest items on the skin care scene. You'll find out what's hot and why. If you'd like an in-depth look at your skin, click on Skin Care 101. You'll get information on **Skin Science**, **Taking Care of Your Skin**, and **Factors Affecting Your Skin**.

Now, let's click on over to the Cosmetics Counter. You've already seen some of the luscious colours in **Virtual Look** and **My Assessment**. How about if we go over and click on What's Hot in Cosmetics. Oh, yes! That was a good move. Here you'll see several different looks created with the season's newest colours. Pick the one you like the best and you'll find everything you need to know to recreate that look at home. Right down to which colours to use where.

Before we leave **My Self**, let's brush up a bit on all the right make-up moves. Click on Cosmetics 101 to find **Application Tips** galore. You'll see pointers on **Basic Application**, **Contouring**, looks for **Career**, **Casual**, **Evening**, **Bridal**, **Teens**, and more. There's also some advice on **Selecting Products** with special emphasis on **Colour** and **Foundation**.

If you're looking for a certain type of product, go back to the **Cosmetics Counter** and you'll find everything you need there. Choose from **Foundations**, **Concealers**, **Powders**, **Blush**, **Eye Make-up**, **Lip Colour**, and **Nail Colour**. You'll even find **Accessories**, like **Nail Colour Remover**, **Compacts** and **Sharpeners**.

You should be feeling pretty good by now. Just knowing that you have a staff of experts nearby to steer you in the right direction is enough to help you relax a little. If you want to feel truly pampered, we suggest you try one more little click before you go. And yes, in some ways, we've saved the best for last. Click on Aromatherapy to discover what everybody's talking about.

You'll find just what you need here to take on another day.
Heavenly **Aromatherapy Systems**, made with natural essential
oils, will help put your life back into perspective. Soothe your
senses. Uplift your mood. Restore inner harmony. Ignite your
love life. And while you're creating sparks, light a match to one of
the **Aromatherapy Candles** and let your light shine!

CLICK 8   HOT BUYS

CLICK HERE TO FIND SOME OF THE BEST DEALS AROUND. TOP QUALITY MERCHANDISE. AT LOW PRICES. ALL WITH QUIXTAR'S CUSTOMER SATISFACTION GUARANTEE. SO YOU NEVER HAVE TO WORRY ABOUT WHAT YOU'RE GETTING. DON'T DELAY. CLICK TODAY. BECAUSE WHAT YOU SEE HERE MAY BE GONE TOMORROW. GET THEM WHILE THEY'RE HOT.

HOT BUYS

REAL DEALS

Have you ever picked up a sale flyer from your local newspaper and seen some really great deals advertised? Recently, a friend of ours showed up at a sale like this. She got there early in the morning, before the sun was even up. She was amazed to find a long line of shoppers waiting outside in the cold winter weather for the store to open its doors. As soon as the doors were unlocked, she fought the crowd and managed to get to the department where they had the item she wanted. Or should we say where the item used to be. Just moments before she arrived, the last one had been loaded into another shopper's cart and was headed to the checkout.

Aren't you glad to know that there's a better way? If you're looking for an especially good deal, you'll find **Hot Buys** right here, 24 hours a day. And you won't get trampled on your way to the checkout.

These items are covered by the **Quixtar Exclusives** satisfaction guarantee. You won't find any seconds or defects here. This is top quality merchandise. So you can shop with confidence.

When you see something you like in **Hot Buys**, you'd better give it a quick click and head straight to the checkout. These items are in short supply and they won't last long. We learned this lesson the hard way when we saw something we liked but browsed around a bit before we came back to put it in our shopping cart. Sure enough, by the time we returned, it was gone.

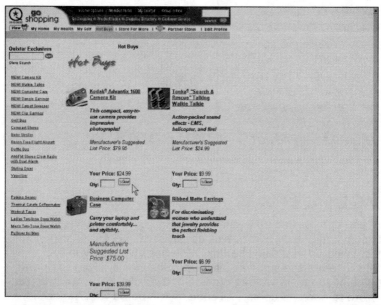

FIGURE 8-1   HOT BUYS

You'll also notice that the number of offerings in **Hot Buys** is rather limited. There may only be a few dozen items here to choose from. Don't let that discourage you. Get them while they're hot.

On a recent visit to **Hot Buys**, we found electronics like video games, televisions, stereos, clock radios, telephones, cameras, and personal data organizers. Kitchen appliances were there, too, with a bread machine, microwave, slow cooker, and a programmable digital coffeemaker. Grooming products shown included a hot air brush, electric toothbrush and a cordless shaver. There were leather goods, luggage and watches for men and women. Even the kids got into the act with an electric train set, an infant toy set, and a remote-controlled racecar.

Where Have All the PVs Gone? IBOs will notice that the items in **Hot Buys** have less PV/BV attached to them than usual. This is because the prices are so low that they can't place as many points on them. We know you'll appreciate having the extra savings up front.

You'll see all the **Hot Buy** items listed down the side of your screen. Make sure you scroll all the way down to get a look at every last one of them. You can get to the item you want by clicking on the name of the item in the list. That will take you right to the page that the item is pictured on. When you see something you like, click on the picture and you'll see a bigger picture with an expanded description of the item. You can drop it into your shopping cart now by clicking the Add button. Or, click the More Info button to zoom in on the picture.

Scroll Back in the days of King Arthur, people used to get messages on a long scroll of parchment. The entire sheet was too long to be seen at once, so the messenger would have to unroll the ends of the scroll, inch by inch, to be able to see the rest of the message. Today, we have to scroll down on our computer screens to see the entire web page. You can do this with a scroll wheel on your mouse, with the down arrow on your keyboard, or by dragging the arrows that appear on the right side of your screen. If you can't quite get the hang of it, ask your five or seven-year-old. They'll show you.

If you'd rather browse by looking at all the pictures, scroll down to the bottom of the page and you'll see all the page numbers listed there, from left to right across your screen. Click on the first set of pages to see the first group of **Hot Buys**. Then, go back down to the page numbers and click on the next set of page numbers to see a different group of pictures. You can go through all the pages like this to be sure you see everything. It won't take long, because **Hot Buys** are very limited.

You're sure to find something you like each time you visit **Hot Buys.**

CLICK 9   STORE FOR MORE^{SM}

CLICK HERE TO OPEN THE DOORS TO YOUR FAVORITE STORE. THE STORE FOR MORE. MORE OF THE THINGS YOU WANT. MORE OF THE BRANDS YOU TRUST. FASHION. CONVENIENCE. ELECTRONICS. FOR YOUR HOME. YOUR FAMILY. YOUR LIFE. IT'S ALL HERE FOR YOU AT THE STORE FOR MORE. COME ON IN. YOU'LL LOVE WHAT YOU SEE.

STORE FOR MORE^{SM}

YOUR FAVORITE STORE

There was a time and a place where you could shop for practically everything you needed under one roof. It was a friendly store. They knew your name. They cared about you. And about your family. They stood behind their merchandise. Gave you service with a smile. And you always felt better when you went back home. Today, that store is back. It's called the **Store For More**.

When you enter the **Store For More**, you'll find thousands of items from hundreds of name-brand manufacturers. Names you know and trust. The products you want most. All under one roof.

There's More Where That Came From   This will be your favorite store for more than one reason. IBOs will find that **Store For More** items almost always come with higher PV/BV than items found in Partner Stores. So remember to check here first for whatever you need.

Like a big department store, you'll find the things you need grouped into sections to make your shopping easier. Unlike those big stores in town, you won't have to fight for a parking space or wear yourself out walking up and down the aisles looking for what you want. Everything is just a click away.

FIGURE 9-1 STORE FOR MORE

FASHION

Have you ever gone into a big store and asked where you could find the ladies' dresses? Chances are, you were told that the career dresses were in one spot, the evening dresses up a floor, the sportswear over there, the women's sizes downstairs, the petites on the mezzanine, and the designer dresses each have their own separate department. Sometimes it just seems like too much trouble and you may decide you don't really want a dress after all. Why, for goodness sake, can't they just put all the dresses together?

You'll be glad to know that you can easily find the dress you're looking for at the **Store For More**. Click on Fashion and you'll see **Women's** listed along with other groups like **Men's** and **Children's**. Go ahead and click on Women's since you're looking for a dress. Now you'll see different types of fashions for women – groups like **Casual Wear**, **Sweaters**, **Outerwear**, **Intimate Apparel**, **Shoes**, **Accessories**, and yes, **Dress Wear**.

You know what do to next, click on Dress Wear. Now you'll see pictures of dresses for you to look at. Aren't they nice and easy to look at? No racks crowded with dress after dress, no dresses falling off the hangers, no running from floor to floor. They're all right here. Scroll down the page until you find one that catches your eye. If you want to see more, you'll find additional page numbers at the bottom of your screen, from left to right. Click on the next one to move to the next group of pictures. Or, if you prefer, you can scan the list of items on the side of the page. When you see one that you'd like to look at, just click on the description and you'll go right to it.

Now, that one sounds nice, a Two-piece Crepe Dress. Let's click that one and have a closer look. Oh, that looks great! An elegant satin-trimmed jacket with satin-covered buttons and an elastic skirt with a back zipper. Beautiful details. But of course, it's from Jessica Howard. And look at the price! Only $87.00. Now, that's just perfect. Click the little arrow to choose your size and desired color. And one more click to Add to Basket. What a pleasant way to shop!

Next, you'll see your **Shopping Cart**. Click Check Out if you're ready or click Return to Shopping if you want to look some more.

CONVENIENCE

Here's a section you'll really appreciate. There's all kinds of stuff here that you need, but just dread lugging home from the store. Because a lot of these things are heavy. Things like **Pet Food, Beverages**, and **Trash Bags**. You'll also find everyday essentials like **Batteries, Beauty Care, Cleaners, Food Storage, Health Care, Meals, Medications**, and **Snacks**. Lighten your load by moving right from click to ship, and before you know it, these heavy items will be at your front door. Now that's **Convenience**.

ELECTRONICS

Calling all gadget gurus, don't miss this! You'll find hours of enjoyment here in the **Electronics** section of the **Store For More**. Whether you're looking for **Camcorders, Cameras, Car Stereos, DVD Players, Fax Machines, Telephones, Televisions, VCRs**, or **WebTV®,** you'll find them right here.

Let's Go Surfin' Now Catch the e-commerce wave, even if you don't have a computer. How? With **WebTV®**, from the **Store For More**. You can surf the site, send & receive email, and do e-commerce. No need to make a big investment, you're in business for just a couple hundred bucks. You can be crusin' the site with **WebTV®**, right from your favorite easy chair.

You can even get Major Appliances like Whirlpool® Washers and Dryers, Ranges, Dishwashers, Compactors and Microwaves.

HOME

You'll find something for every room in your **Home** in this department. Come on in and see the wonderful selections for your **Bedroom, Bathroom, Baby's Room, Kitchen, Dining Room**, and **Office**. Make your life a bit easier with **Kitchen Essentials**, and **Kitchen Appliances, Large** or **Small**. You'll even find equipment to help you **Exercise**, along with **Automotive** stuff and items for the **Garage** and **Laundry**. Don't forget to look in **Home Accents** where you'll find cozy afghans and throws to snuggle up with on a chilly evening. Even the **Furniture** is here, at the **Store For More**.

SEASONAL

When the weather outside is frightful, you'll find **Holiday** shopping just delightful in this department of the **Store For More**. Fix yourself a cup of hot cocoa and stay home where it's nice and warm. Let Santa make his list and check it twice. You'll be able to click your list away in just a few short hours.

Everything you need for a bright **Holiday** season can be delivered to your door. You'll find **Toys** and **Gifts** for everyone on your list. The kids will love opening up packages with **Dolls and Stuffed Animals, Games and Puzzles, Toy Trucks and Cars, Books and Activity Kits**, and even **Educational Toys**. Grown-ups will appreciate the **Inspirational Gifts, Sweets and Treats, Designer Fragrances and Cologne, Calendars, Music, Videos, DVD**, and more. Your home will look festive with these **Trees and Wreaths, Ornaments, Decorations**, and **Gift Wrap**, too. Relax, the **Holiday** season will be a breeze with **The Store For More** on your side. The **Holiday** items are generally available from September through January.

And when Spring has sprung, you'll find everything you need to get ready for the warm weather ahead, right here at **The Store For More**.   Why spend your weekend out fighting the crowds to find the perfect gear for your summer fun? The **Store For More** is full of all the things you'll need to enjoy a fun-filled summer. Click here for **Camping Equipment, Pool Equipment and Supplies, Bicycles, Golf Equipment**, and **Lawn and Garden Care and Equipment**.

Why lug home heavy stuff like patio furniture, garden and pool supplies, swing sets, and barbecue grills? The **Store For More** has a wonderful selection of these items, and much more. And they'll deliver it right to your front door. After all, summertime should be a time when the living is easy!

HOT BUYS

You'll find the same **Hot Buys** in this department that you've seen in the **Quixtar Exclusives**. The same great merchandise. At the same low prices. Just one more way for you to scoop up these deals while supplies last!

Now Isn't That Special   In each department of the **Store For More**, you'll find a link to the **Specials** for that department. Here's a great place to save a few dollars on some really good stuff. Stop by often, to see which items are being offered as **Specials** today.

GET CATALOG

Pssst! Over here! We're going to let you in on a little secret. All those wonderful things you found at the **Store For More**. That's just the tip of the iceberg. There's more. A lot more. And you can find the rest of it by ordering a catalog from the **Get Catalog** part of this site.

Choose from the **Personal Shoppers**® Catalog, the **Jewelry and Fragrance** Catalog, a Catalog of CD-ROMs called **Knowledge and Learning**, and an **Office and Janitorial Catalog**. There are even seasonal catalogs – a **Christmas Catalog** and a **Spring/Summer Catalog**.

To order your catalogs, just click on the red Get Catalog link at the top of your screen. Find the ones you want, click on the picture of the catalog cover, and then click Add to Basket. Members and Clients can order single copies of catalogs. IBOs will find catalogs available in packs of three or ten. You'll be turning the pages in no time!

CUSTOMER SERVICE

You can shop with confidence from the **Store For More** because your purchases are backed by a **Full One-Year Warranty.** You'll find details on the **Guarantee and Warranty** here in **Customer Service.** You'll also get the specifics on **Postage Costs.** Find instructions for **Repairs, Damaged or Defective Merchandise,** and **Returns** (they're easy, and you don't have to pay the shipping). Learn how **Back Orders** are processed and more. **Customer Service Representatives** are standing by to answer your questions. You can even **Phone Toll-Free** to reach them, or **Write** them a letter or **E-Mail.**

To reach **Customer Service,** click on the red Customer Service link at the top of your screen and select More Help. Or call, 1-800-222-1462.

SFM HOME PAGE

If you've ever gotten lost in a big department store and couldn't find your way back out to the front door, you'll like this feature. Just click on the red SFM Home Page link at the top of your screen to go back to where you entered the store.

SHOPPING CART

Take a peek into your shopping cart any time you like. Click on the View Cart icon in the red square at the top of your screen. You'll see the **Shopping Cart** page that shows you each item in your cart, the **Quantity,** stock number, size and color, **PV/BV** for IBOs, the **Item Retail** price and the **Item Cost.** If you are purchasing for someone other than yourself, Select a purchase mode at the top of the page. Next, click in the red Check Out box.

Now, you'll see the **Shipping Information** screen. Verify that all your information appears correctly. If you want to Ship to Another IBO, click in that box and then type **Their IBO#** in the box provided. Click in the red Check Out box.

Now you'll see the **Shipping Options** screen with the details about how your order will be shipped. Click on Check Out.

The next screen is called **Order Preview**. This is where you'll want to scrutinize your order to make sure everything appears exactly the way you want it. Complete your **Payment Information** by clicking either Credit Card or Bank Draft. Bank Draft is only offered to those who have previously been approved. Type in your **Name**, **Card Number**, and select your Card Type and Expiration date from the drop-down boxes. When you are ready, click in the red Purchase box.

You'll now see the **Order Confirmation** screen. It will have your **Invoice No**. You can print out a copy of this for your records if you like. It really isn't necessary, though. Go check your email and you'll find that a message has already arrived for you!

This is your **Quixtar Order Confirmation**. It details your order for you once again. It even contains a link to let you View Your Order. Click on this link and, after you pass by your **Login**, it will take you to the **Order History** section in **Customer Service**. And there it is! The top **Invoice #** on your list is the order that you just placed moments ago. Amazing!

If you'd like to enjoy this thrill for a few moments more, click on the Invoice #. You'll see the **Order Detail**, including the date and time you placed your order. Look at your watch. That's fast! But what would you expect from the Store For More?

CLICK 10 · PARTNER STORES

CLICK HERE TO DISCOVER THE MULTITUDE OF TOP-BRAND STORES THAT OFFER YOU DIRECT LINKS TO THEIR SITES, GOOD PRICING, AND SECURE PURCHASING. ALL THIS PLUS Q-CREDITS FOR QUIXTAR MEMBERS AND PV/BV FOR QUIXTAR IBOS! COME ON OVER AND SEE WHAT ALL THE EXCITEMENT IS ABOUT.

PARTNER STORES

SHOPPING SHORTCUTS

There's a gigantic shopping mall in our hometown. It has over two million square feet of retail space. The parking lot is huge. Each section of the lot is named after an animal and then there are row numbers, just like in a big amusement park, so you can find where you parked your car. But as shoppers, we are not amused. They have a staff of security officers who ride around in little vehicles, just helping people look for their cars. You can wear out a pair of shoes there in just one day. It's exhausting.

Compare that shopping experience to the stores you have to choose from on this site. Do you realize you have more stores to choose from in **Partner Stores** than you'd have if you went to that mammoth shopping mall? And you'll never have to walk further than your own home.

The **Partner Store** shops are grouped into categories, like **Food & Gifts, Home & Family, Office & Technical, Sports**

& Leisure, and **More**. Click on any of these categories and you'll get a list of links to the shops in that group.

Let's give it a whirl. Begin at the navy blue navigational bar. Click on Go Shopping, then click on Partner Stores. Next, pick the category of stores you'd like to visit. Let's click on Office & Technology.

FIGURE 10-1   PARTNER STORE PAGE

The next screen you'll see is the one that links you to the sites of the Partner Stores in the category you chose. Look over the list and pick one that you like. Let's click on OfficeMax. Now, you'll see a screen that gives you a brief description of the merchandise the store carries. At OfficeMax, you'll see that they have over 20,000 office products and offer free next business-day delivery. IBOs will also see the PV/BV percentages they'll earn when they shop at this Partner Store. Members will see the amount of

Q-Credits they'll earn there. Go ahead and click on Visit OfficeMax Website.

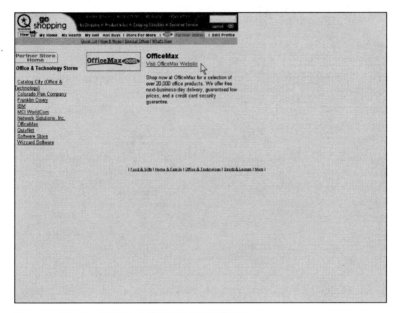

FIGURE 10-2   LINK TO OFFICE MAX SITE

Enter Here   To earn Q-Credits or PV/BV from Partner Stores, you must enter every store through the **Quixtar** site. If you hop from shop to shop, be sure you go back to **Quixtar** in between and enter the next shop from there. That way you'll enjoy all the benefits you deserve.

Wow! Look at that! There's the OfficeMax site. But this version of the OfficeMax site is customized for Quixtar IMCs. You'll see that the Quixtar **Go Shopping** navigational bar is still at the top of your screen.

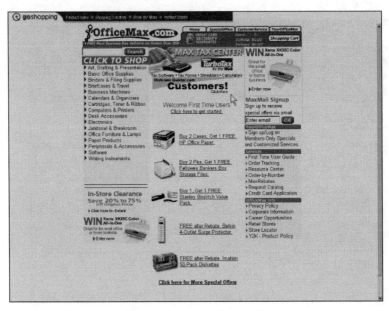

FIGURE 10-3   OFFICEMAX PARTNER STORE SITE

Once inside a **Partner Store**, you'll enjoy all it has to offer. It will provide you with a shopping cart, process your order, ship it, and handle any returns. *Take a few minutes to look into the policies and procedures of any store where you shop. Each store has its own customer service information to give you all the details.*

Who's Keeping Score? Each **Partner Store** is required to track your purchases and report them back to **Quixtar**. Q-Credits or PV/BV will be awarded to you within 60 days of purchase. IBOs can stop by **Virtual Office** to see their volume and Members can see their Q-Credits in **My Quixtar**.

QUICK LIST

Click on Quick List to see an alphabetical list of Partner Stores. You'll also see how much PV/BV IBOs will receive on their orders and on orders of Members. And Members can look here to see how many Q-Credits they will receive for each dollar spent.

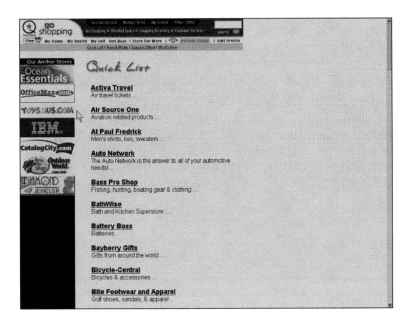

FIGURE 10-4   QUICK LIST PAGE

Here is a summary of the **Quick List**. *Anchor Stores* are shown in italics:

Partner Store	Type of Merchandise	PV/BV% on IBO Orders	PV/BV% on Member Orders	Q-Credits per $ spent
Activa Travel	Air travel tickets	5/10	2.5/5	3
Air Source One	Aviation related products	10/20	5/10	7
At Paul Fredrick	Men's shirts, ties, sweaters	11/22	5.5/11	8
AutoNetwork (Amounts given are for Auto Club Total Plan. Other services carry different amounts.)	Automotive needs	50/100	25/50	3500
Bass Pro Shop	Fishing, hunting, boating gear & clothing	6/12	3/6	4
BathWise	Bath & Kitchen Superstore	10/20	5/10	7
Battery Boss	Batteries	14/28	7/14	10
Bayberry Gifts	Gifts from around the world	19/38	9.5/19	13
Bicycle Central	Bicycles & accessories	19/38	9.5/19	13
Bite Footwear & Apparel	Golf shoes, sandals & apparel	24/48	12/24	17
BodyRelief	Relaxation products	11/22	5.5/11	7
Catalog City	Hundreds of catalogs online	10/20	5/10	7

Partner Store	Type of Merchandise	PV/BV% on IBO Orders	PV/BV% on Member Orders	Q-Credits per $ spent
CD Universe	CDs, Cassettes, VHS, LD, & DVD	19/38	9.5/19	13
Chocoholic	Premium chocolates	14/28	7/14	10
Clearwater Seafood	Specialty seafood dinners	10/20	5/10	7
Collectible Toyz Store	Collectible toys, b-babies, etc.	19/38	9.5/19	13
Colorado Pen Company	Pens	14/28	7/14	10
Diamond Jeweler	Gold jewelry & diamonds	23/46	11.5/23	16
Doll House Shoppe	Dolls, dollhouses & accessories	19/38	9.5/19	13
Drug Free Home	Drug education	19/38	9.5/19	13
eSportsonline	Sporting goods	11/22	5.5/11	8
Finding Time, Inc.	Healthcare & Medical products	10/20	5/10	7
First Alert Professional Security (One time PV/BV & Q-Credits awarded at sign-up)	Home security systems	50	100	10,000
FloraGift	Floral & gifts	19/38	9.5/19	13

Partner Store	Type of Merchandise	PV/BV% On IBO Orders	PV/BV% On Member Orders	Q-Credits Per $ spent
Franklin Covey	Planners, organizers	19/38	9.5/19	13
Franklin Mint	Collectibles & Heirloom Works of Art	10/20	5/10	
Front Door Foods	Specialty foods	10/20	5/10	7
Fuller Brush Company	Homecare equipment	38/76	19/38	27
Game Store	All types of games	14/28	7/14	10
GetBulbs	Thousands of light bulbs	11/22	5.5/11	8
Golf Gifts by Southern Appeal	Golf gift items	11/22	5.5/11	8
Great Food	Specialty food items	10/20	5/10	7
Hardware.com	Home improvement products	10/20	5/10	7
Hickory Farms	Specialty food & gifts	14/28	7/14	10
Home Shoppe	Home decorative products	14/28	7/14	10
IBM	Computer hardware, software & more	10/20	5/10	7
IGO GOLF	Golf clubs & accessories	10/20	5/10	7
Justrims	Tires & wheels	31/62	15.5/31	22
Keepsakes and Memories	Jewelry, gifts & collectibles	24/48	12/24	17

Partner Store	Type of Merchandise	PV/BV% on IBO Orders	PV/BV% on Member Orders	Q-Credits per $ spent
Knives and Collectibles	Collectible knives & more	19/38	9.5/19	13
KrazyCrabcakes Gourmet Foods Development	Specialty crabcakes	24/48	12/24	17
Landscape USA	Lawn & garden supplies	14/28	7/14	10
Leather Goods Depot	Leather products	19/38	9.5/19	13
Lens Express	Contact lenses & sunglasses	10/20	5/10	7
LifeLine-USA	Fitness training devices	29/58	14.5/29	20
Lionel Trains	Toy trains	14/28	7/14	10
Magellan's	Luggage & travel items	10/20	5/10	7
Matter of Time	Watches	24/48	12/24	17
MCI WorldCom (One time PV/BV & Q-Credits awarded at sign-up)	Long distance service	100	100	2000
Network Solutions, Inc.	Domain name registration	33/66	16.5/33	23
Nice Shades and Things	Sunglasses & more	19/38	9.5/19	13

Partner Store	Type of Merchandise	PV/BV% on IBO Orders	PV/BV% on Member Orders	Q-Credits per $ spent
Ocean Essentials (In addition to PV/BV, IBOs also earn 7.5% of the retail price in cash on IBO purchases only)	Nutritional supplements	30/75	30/75	15
OfficeMax	Office supplies	6/12	3/6	4
Omaha Steaks	Steaks, seafood & desserts	14/28	7/14	10
Outlet Tool Supply	Power, air & hand tools	14/28	7/14	10
Premium Steaks	Specialty beef	10/20	5/10	7
ProTeam	Licensed sports attire	14/28	7/14	10
QuixNet (PV/BV & Q-Credits awarded for each month of paid service)	Family-friendly ISP	2.5/5 per month	2.5/5 per month	200 per month
Shopping. Hollywood.com	Entertainment studio store	10/20	5/10	7
Silver Mine	Silver jewelry & gemstones	29/58	14.5/29	20
Software Store	Computer software	14/28	7/14	10
Sports Collector's Haven	Licensed MLB & NFL merchandise	14/28	7/14	10
Superior Coffee	Coffee, tea & gifts	11/22	5.5/11	8

Partner Store	Type of Merchandise	PV/BV% on IBO Orders	PV/BV% on Member Orders	Q-Credits per $ spent
The Phone Connection	Vintage collectible phones	14/28	7/14	10
The Tire Place	All types of tires	26-32PV 52-64 BV	13-16 PV 26-32 BV	18-23
Totally Fun Toys	Educational toys	11/22	5.5/11	8
ToysRus.com	The hottest toys, the greatest deals!	11/22	5.5/11	8
WebClothes.com	Children's apparel	14/28	7/14	10
Wizzard Software	Interactive voice software	24/48	12/24	17
Yo-Yo City	Yo-yos & more	10/20	5/10	7

©2000. Quixtar, Inc. Grand Rapids, MI. March 24, 2000.
Partner Store and other information subject to change without notice.

Open Up! When you first click on a Partner Store from **Quick List** or the category page, you'll see a screen that tells you what type of items they carry and how many Q-Credits or PV/BV you'll earn for shopping there. Just click on the store's name & they'll let you in.

HOW IT WORKS

Once you get the hang of it, you'll be zipping in and out of **Partner Stores** so fast it will make your mouse spin. In the beginning, it'd be a good idea for you to click on How It Works to get some pointers on navigating the **Partner Stores** sites. That way, you'll get the lay of the land and you won't run into any roadblocks along the way.

Navigational Bar   A Navigational Bar is a tool that helps you find your way around a website. You'll usually find it at the top or bottom of each page or screen. Quixtar uses a navy blue bar across the top of your screen as its Navigational Bar. Just click on any of the words in the navy blue bar and you'll jump right to that section of the site.

Don't Touch That Dial   As you travel through the Partner Stores, keep an eye out for that navy blue **Navigational Bar**. If it disappears from your screen, use your Back button until it shows up again. That bar is your assurance that your purchases are earning you Q-Credits or PV/BV.

SPECIAL OFFERS

Partner Stores sometimes run **Special Offers** to encourage you to visit their site. Click on Special Offers to find out which sites are running these special deals. These offers are usually only good for a few weeks, so take advantage of them while they last. A recent visit to **Special Offers** found additional discounts on Palm™ products, a free gift certificate offer for fresh seafood, an extra savings on all purchases made at a certain Partner Store, and temporarily increased PV/BV at another Partner Store.

Do the "Back-Button Dance"   If you ever encounter an error message you don't like, just do the "Back-Button Dance". Click on the Back button on your browser. Then, whatever you clicked on before that gave you that error, click on it again. Usually, you'll sail right through the next time. If not, click the Back button again, and go back and forth until you get through. That's the "Back-Button Dance"!

REWARDS BROCHURE

Partner Stores are being added to the site all the time. To be sure you stay current on all the shopping sites available to you, click on Rewards Brochure, at the top of your screen. To access an up-to-date summary of all the **Partner Stores**, go to the bottom of your screen and Click here to view the Partner Stores Reward Brochure.

When you do, Adobe® Acrobat® Reader will be launched and you'll be able to view a brochure that lists the **Partner Stores** in each **Category**, like **Food & Gifts**, **Home & Family**, **Office & Technology**, **Sports & Leisure**, and **More**. IBOs will see the PV/BV percentages they'll earn on their Partner Store purchases and those of their Members. Members will see the Q-Credits that will be awarded to them for each dollar spent at a **Partner Store**.

WHAT'S NEW

Each month, you'll find an update on new **Partner Stores** that have been added by clicking on What's New. You'll also hear about new catalogs that have been added to **Catalog City**.

What's **Catalog City**? We're so glad you asked...

CLICK 11   CATALOG CITY

CLICK HERE TO FIND THE ONLINE VERSION OF HUNDREDS OF MAIL-ORDER CATALOGS. LEISURELY BROWSE THROUGH YOUR FAVORITE CATALOG PAGE-BY-PAGE OR ZOOM-IN USING A POWERFUL SEARCH FEATURE TO FIND EXACTLY WHAT YOU'RE LOOKING FOR. DOG-EARED PAGES ARE A THING OF THE PAST WHEN YOU USE CATALOG CITY'S HANDY REMINDER FEATURE TO KEEP TRACK OF THINGS YOU DON'T NEED TO ORDER TODAY BUT MIGHT NEED WEEKS FROM NOW. SO TOSS OUT THE CATALOGS THAT CLUTTER YOUR COUNTERS. ORDER THROUGH THE CATALOG CITY PARTNER STORE INSTEAD. MEMBERS WILL EARN Q-CREDITS AND IBOS WILL EARN PV/BV.

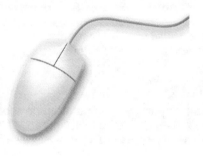

CATALOG CITY

WELCOME TO CATALOG CITY

Okay, we admit it. We're catalog junkies! Our home has piles and piles of catalogs. And they multiply faster than rabbits. When we discovered this site, we were thrilled. Many of our favorite catalogs are now online!

To get to **Catalog City**, begin at the navy blue navigational bar. Click on Go Shopping, and then click on Partner Stores. Look on the left side of your screen and you'll see big icons for the Partner Store Anchors. Click on the icon for Catalog City. Then click on the link for Visit Catalog City Website. The next screen you'll see will be the **Welcome to Catalog City**.

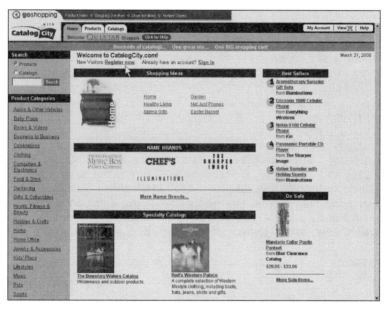

FIGURE 11-1   WELCOME TO CATALOG CITY

When you shop at **Catalog City**, you're always greeted by name. So the first thing you'll want to do is to click on Register Now. That will take you to the **Sign In** screen. Just fill in your information and create a password. Click the Sign In button and you're on your way. Now, every time you re-enter the **Catalog City** Partner Store site, you'll be greeted by name. And when you place an order, they'll know where to ship it to you.

At the top of your screen, just below Quixtar's navy blue navigational bar, you'll see Catalog City's green navigational bar. It has tabs for **Home**, **Products**, and **Catalogs**, as well as buttons for **My Account**, **View Cart**, and **Help**. Click on the Home tab, and you'll see several choices drop down: **Welcome**, **About Catalog City**, **Privacy Policy**, and **Safe Shopping Guarantee**. We're going to skip over these for now, but you can come back later and explore them if you're interested.

PRODUCTS

Go ahead and click on the Products tab. Notice you now have drop-down choices for **Categories**, **What's New**, **What's Hot**, and **On Sale**. When you click on one of these choices, you'll see the color change from black to blue. That way, you'll always know which page you're on. Start by clicking on Categories.

Here you'll find categories like **Clothing, Entertainment, Gardening, Home**, and **Travel**, just to name a few. Pick the one you want and click on it. If you choose Clothing, the next screen you'll see shows you the subcategories for **Clothing**, like **Boys', Designer, Girls', Men's, Women's** and so on. Click on Women's and you'll find various types of apparel for women: **blazers, casual shoes, dress shoes, dresses, pants, skirts, suits**, etc. Just keep clicking on items until you zero in on what you want. If you click on dress shoes, you'll see a page that shows you pictures of dress shoes.

Just above the first picture, you'll see a box that says **Show**. Click the drop-down arrow in this box and you'll be given several different ways you can view the shoes on this page. You can choose to view them by price or by name. You can also choose to see 10, 20, or 50 items at a time. The more items you see at a time, the smaller the pictures will be. Click on your preference and then click Go. Just above the **Show** box, you'll see the total number of items available in that category. In this case, we saw (1-10 of 61), meaning we were looking at the first 10 pictures out of a total of 61. To see the next batch of pictures, scroll down to the bottom of the pictures and click on Next.

FIGURE 11-2 SHOPPING FOR SHOES

Now, back to shoe shopping! Look at the pictures until you find one you like. How about an Asymmetrical Slingback Sandal for $56.00? Click on either the picture or the description, and you will jump to a larger picture with a more detailed description. You can either click Add to Cart or Save to Gift Registry. Since you're buying these for yourself, click Add to Cart. Next, specify your size and color choice, and click OK. They come in black, pewter, olive and purple. Since this is such a great basic, at such a great price, why not get one in every color!

Your Shopping Cart will be the next page you see. Each item you've added to your cart will be shown here, along with the catalog they came from, the quantity, price, size and color. Over on the right, you'll see **Options**. This is where you can choose to **Change, Remove**, or **Save for Later**. If you click Save for Later, that item will move down to a separate section at the bottom of your screen. Later, when you are ready to purchase it, click Move to Cart and it will go back into your cart at the top.

You will find two buttons at the bottom of your cart – **Continue shopping** and **Checkout**. The total dollar amount of merchandise you have in your cart will be shown here as well. Click Checkout and you'll move to the **Validate** screen. Here, you'll enter your **password** and choose a checkout aisle. Use the **EXPRESS Checkout** if you are shipping to your own address and charging to a credit card you've used at **Catalog City** before. This aisle allows you to skip over the **Ship To** and **Payment** screens. The other **Checkout** accepts coupons, gift certificates, allows you to add gift cards, ship to any address, and pay with any credit card. If this is your first visit to **Catalog City**, click Checkout.

Now you're at the **Ship To** screen. Type in the **address** you want to ship to and select the shipping method – **Standard** or **Express**. If you want to enclose a card, click in the Gift card box and click Continue. On the next screen, enter your **Payment** information and click Continue. If you requested a gift card, complete the message now and click Continue.

It's time to review your order for accuracy and click Submit Order. You will be given an order number immediately. Also, a confirmation of your order will be sent to your e-mail address.

CATALOGS

While some people prefer to shop for specific **Products**, there are those of us who'd rather shop by store. If you're one of those people, click on the Catalogs tab. Now you'll have a choice of tabs for **Categories**, **A-Z Index**, **Name Brands**, and **Specialty Brands**. When you click on A-Z Index, on the left side of your screen you'll see alphabetical groupings, like A-C, D-F, G-I, etc. If you'd like to look up a certain catalog alphabetically, this is where you'll find it. Some of the shops you'll find here will be familiar to you from your local shopping malls. Some of your favorite mail-order catalogs will be here, too. And you'll find plenty of new names to explore as well.

Let's say you're shopping for a gift for your father. You'd rather steer clear of clothing this time because he just went on a cruise and may have put on a few extra pounds. How about a gadget of some sort? Like the kind of stuff they have at The Sharper Image.

Let's see if The Sharper Image is on the site. Click on the
Catalogs tab. Now look on the left side of your screen, in the wide
green bar, and you'll see the alphabetical ranges. Click on S-U.
There it is! Click on The Sharper Image.

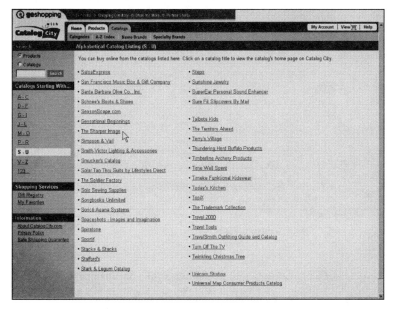

FIGURE 11-3   CATALOG CITY A-Z INDEX

You're sure to find something unique for him here. Look, they
have 227 items to choose from. Browse through the online
catalog. You can even view the items by price, if you want. Or,
go right to the **Sale Items**. Over to the left, in the wide green
bar. Click on Sale Items. How about those 8x32 Waterproof
Binoculars? They're reduced from $179.00 to $149.95. Dad
would really appreciate those beauties. He could take them on his
next fishing trip. Or into the football stadium, to catch all the
plays, rain or shine.

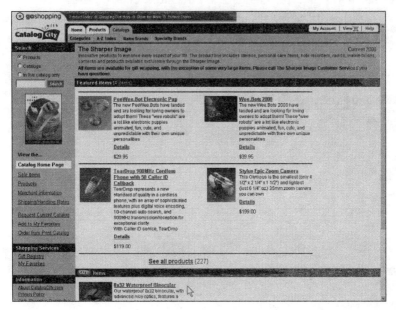

FIGURE 11-4 THE SHARPER IMAGE

When you click on Categories, you'll see a list of categories that looks just like the list you saw a few minutes ago when you were in **Products**. But this time, it works differently. Click on Clothing, then on Women's Clothing.

This time, you'll see pictures of **Catalog** covers instead of pictures of **Products**. All of these catalogs contain **Women's Clothing**. Browse through until you find one that you like and then click. How about The Territory Ahead? Click the catalog cover and you'll go to the **Catalog Home Page**.

At the top, you'll see their **Featured Items**. Usually, there are just a few things here to give you an idea of the type of merchandise they carry. Just below that, you'll see **See all products**, followed by a number in parenthesis. In this case, you'll see that they have 186 items.

To see more items, click on one of these See all links. Now set
your Show box to 10, 20, or 50, and start browsing. You know
what to do from here on out. There is another way to browse the
catalog, though, and this is probably our favorite. Look in the
green column on the left. Now, click on Catalog Pages. Isn't that
cool? What you see is the print catalog, with pages displayed
side-by-side, just like you would if you were sitting on your sofa
turning them yourself.

You'll see a brief description of what's on each page, next to the
picture. When you want to take a closer look, click on Zoom
In/Buy Products. This is even better than having the paper
catalog, because there's no clutter on your countertops. If you do
want a catalog though, you can click on Request Current Catalog,
over there in the green column. Look over the other features in
that list, too. You can get **Merchant Information**, **Gift
Registry**, **Shipping Rates**, sometimes **Order from Print
Catalog**, and much, much more.

SEARCH

Before you get swept off your feet by what's coming up next,
you'll want to take a few minutes to acquaint yourself with the
Search feature. Because professional shoppers always know
where to find what they're looking for. And you would consider
yourself a professional, right?

When searching this site, or any site, what you want to remember
is "Less is More" and "More is Less". The *more specific* you are
when you type in your search, the fewer results you'll see. The
less specific you are, the more results you'll see.

Try this. Click in the circle next to Products and type in **shoes**.
Shoes is not very specific (less), so you would expect to get a lot
of results (more). And so you do. Somewhere around 767 items,
when we last checked. Now, we don't know about you, but we
aren't going to take the time to look through all those shoes.   Try
something more specific, like **Keds**. Since you are being very
specific (more), you would expect to see fewer pairs (less). And
so you do. Somewhere around 5 items. Leather, canvas, tie, slip-
on, and boat shoes.

So now that you know how to search effectively, when you get more results than what you want, try typing in something more specific. When you get too few, try typing in something less specific. Less is More and More is Less.

A-Z INDEX

Remember seeing an **A-Z Index** tab when you clicked on the **Catalog** tab at the top of your screen? We thought you might like to have a handy reference guide, in print, to refer to, that shows all the catalogs in the **A-Z Index**. So here it is. You can highlight the ones you want to checkout next time you're online. Check back here frequently as new stores are being added all the time.

Here is a summary of the **A-Z Index**:

Store	Type of Merchandise
A&E, The World of	Award winning classic home video entertainment as well as unique gifts for unique tastes.
a.r.t.i.c.l.e.s	Contemporary gifts & décor items to reflect your artistic style, including wire baskets, candles & candleholders, bases, lamps, frames, steel desk sets & cherry wood humidor
ABC Feelings	Fun, interactive communication tools for children & adults, especially designed to help students in discussing & understanding their feelings. Products include posters, coloring books, flash cards, T-shirts, puzzles & placemats.
adaptAbility	Adaptive products to complement an active lifestyle. adaptAbility products are unique & carefully selected to enhance the comfort, safety & quality of life for those with special needs.

Store	Type of Merchandise
The Added Touch	A special atmosphere for the discerning shopper at home & abroad, including a variety of tempting wares, gifts for house & home, gardens, gourmet wines, sports, travel & health.
Advisor Publications	Technical resources for IT professionals & software developers including magazines, CD-ROMs, conferences & online training.
AeroSelect	Select aviation gifts for all ages, including flight jackets, desk clocks, posters, models, books, videos & aviation signs.
African American Gifts	Gifts & collectibles that reflect the African-American heritage including dolls, figurines & sculptures.
Alden Lee Company	Fine hardwood furniture for musicians, including solo, duet, trio & quartet music stands, instrument stands, sheet music storage & player's seating. Alden Lee offers a complete line of music room furniture for home & professional use.
Allergy & Asthma Guide	Products & information to help allergy & asthma sufferers improve the quality of their lives, including filters, HEPA vacuums, bedding, body care products & nebulizers. Many of these products have been recommended by thousands of physicians for over 25 years.
Alpaca Pete's	Alpaca sheepskin products, including area rugs, sweaters, slippers & teddy bears
Alsto's Handy Helpers	Useful "handy helpers" designed to make everyday living easier. Look here for hundreds of great gift ideas that will help beautify a garden, organize a garage, please your pet, or make your pool & patio more relaxing.
AMC Direct	CD duplication technology & advanced media storage products for all your CD-ROM drive, system back-up, printing & long-term storage needs.

Catalog City is adding new catalogs & functionality all the time. This is intended to be a representation of the Catalog City Partner Store site. Please visit the Partner Store to see the current offerings.

Store	Type of Merchandise
America's Pet Door Outlet	Hard-to-find pet doors including sliding glass doors, pet doors for giant breeds, electronic doors, doors designed for walls & sash window pet doors.
American Country Home	Home décor & Holiday products for country living
American Starbuck	Authentically hand-crafted pencil post beds, custom built from a wide variety of woods, including cherry, walnut, oak, mahogany, pine & maple. All beds are expertly finished in a wide range of stained, painted & distressed finishes. There are also five headboard styles & customized frame dimensions to fit any mattress.
The American Tailgater	Everything you need for your pre-game tailgate party. From NFL & NCAA licensed coolers & grills to tents, folding tables & telescoping flagpoles, we have the gear for you!
April Victoria	Gifts & collectibles from the collections of Cicely Mary Barker's Flower Fairies & Beatrix Potter; hand-crafted, scented glycerin soaps & other toiletries; custom-blended teas, cocoas & brownies.
Aquatic Rehabilitation & Therapy Equipment	Aquatic rehabilitation & physical therapy products, including special flotation products, therapy collars, pillows, bells, kickboards, training fins, aqua shoes, apparel & wheelchairs.
Art & Artifact	Diverse objects gleaned from exotic cultures & time periods. Decorative home furnishings & accessories including sculptures, framed prints, carpets, tabletop items, gifts & collectibles. Also included are vintage clothing, fashion accessories & jewelry for men & women.

Catalog City is adding new catalogs & functionality all the time. This is intended to be a representation of the Catalog City Partner Store site. Please visit the Partner Store to see the current offerings.

Store	Type of Merchandise
Art Display Essentials	Display stands, easels, bases, cases & accessories for displaying & protecting your art, antiques & collectibles.
Arthur Beren – Fine Footwear for Women & Men	Fine footwear for men & women presented with our famous commitment to personal service.
Arts From The Orient	Oriental figurines, wall hangings, jewelry, snuff bottles & netsuke. Figurines are made of such materials as ivory, bone, wood, glass, cloisonné, jade & semi-precious stones.
Asia for Kids	A unique collection of materials for parents, teachers & librarians including books, videos, CD-ROMs, dolls, posters, crafts & T-shirts. Learn about the cultures & languages of China, Japan, Korea, Vietnam, Laos, India, the Philippines, Nepal, Indonesia & Asian Americans.
Audio Tech Probe	The Audio Tech Probe Diagnostic Listening Tool for mechanics, technicians & the do-it-yourselfer. The tool accurately pinpoints the source of rattles, leaks & broken parts, making it an excellent diagnostic tool anywhere there is movement of mechanical parts, air, gas or fluids.
Automobilia Limited	A wide variety of fully detailed authentic diecast transportation collectibles.
BackSaver	More than 50 products for health & comfort around the clock, including ergonomic office chairs, computer workstations & zero-gravity recliners.
Bar-F Products	Equine protection products for the horse & rider, including horseboots, protective gear for riders, vests & a kennel mat for your stable dog!

Catalog City is adding new catalogs & functionality all the time. This is intended to be a representation of the Catalog City Partner Store site. Please visit the Partner Store to see the current offerings.

Store	Type of Merchandise
Barrons	All the best dinnerware, giftware & collectibles from the world's foremost manufacturers. In this catalog we've gathered together the best of the best – our top sellers, popular favorites & greatest values – to give you a new look at the most exquisite merchandise available today. Here you can browse through the latest treasures from Lenox, Waterford, Lladro, Swarovski and many others.
Bayberry Gifts	Unique gifts from around the world. Artisans with skills that have been handed down from generations handcraft many of our gifts.
Bear Lake Traders	Join us at the crossroads of emerging spirituality where we offer a collection of personal & spiritual growth products. We honor all traditions with items for home, family, health, work & gifts. Included in this catalog are water fountains, books, CDs, jewelry, meditation & wellness items.
Bilingual Software	Software for language learning & translation.
Birthday Express.com	The most current theme related partyware, favors, activities & toys. This catalog includes everything for your child's party needs from balloons to piñatas, to helpful party tips & information. Let the children's party experts help make your child's next birthday a truly wonderful celebration.
Bits & Pieces	Our collection of jigsaws, mechanical puzzles, electronic games, board games, secret puzzle boxes, mechanical banks & kaleidoscopes. You are certain to find the unique gift for your loved one. Bits & Pieces is the source for puzzles & gifts since 1983.

Catalog City is adding new catalogs & functionality all the time. This is intended to be a representation of the Catalog City Partner Store site. Please visit the Partner Store to see the current offerings.

Store	Type of Merchandise
Black Feather Electronics	Electronics & unusual gifts with products for the home, travel & sports.
Blair Clearance Catalog	A variety of Blair's most popular products – all clearance priced to save you even more money! Items in this catalog are continually changing, so check back often to find great deals on men's & women's clothing & products for your home.
BLAIR Men's Wear	Men's wear, including casual wear, active wear, dress shirts, suits & sport coats. Everything is value-priced – good clothing doesn't have to cost a lot!
Blair Shoppe Gift Gallery	Collectible figurines, pins, artwork for every occasion, including Thomas Kincade, Harley Davidson, Judith G., Boyds Bears & Berta Hummel
Blair Shoppe®	Excellent prices on a vast selection of bedspreads, comforters, sheets, towels, draperies, furniture covers, rugs & giftware.
Bolchazy-Carducci Publishers	Books & audiocassettes for classical studies in Greek & Latin, including textbooks, mythology, references, concordances & cultural studies.
Bombay	Page after page of holiday decorating ideas & gifts for the home. From Nutcrackers & ornaments to candles & holiday décor. Many Bombay items are one-of-a-kind & exclusive, so you won't find them anywhere else.
The Boundary Waters Catalog	Wilderness & outdoor products, including clothing. Thule car top carriers, canoes, gifts & books.
Bright Ideas	A carefully selected collection of materials for the gifted & talented. These products are designed to challenge gifted students in and out of the classroom in all subject areas. There are also many great gift ideas.

Catalog City is adding new catalogs & functionality all the time. This is intended to be a representation of the Catalog City Partner Store site. Please visit the Partner Store to see the current offerings.

Store	Type of Merchandise
Brylane Home	Bedding & window treatments, bath ideas & home furnishings at incredible values all year round.
Buttons	Imported buttons for dressmaking, tailoring, crafts, quilting, wearable art & collectors. These buttons will complement anything you make, wear or exhibit. Buy an extra few and create matching jewelry.
Camellia & Main	A unique collection of home décor. This catalog includes great Christmas gifts for everyone on your list, holiday decorating made easy, and accent furniture for just the right look.
Card Models	Paper model construction kits for creating scale models of castles, buildings, birds, windmills & more. Also includes traditional hobby models such as planes, ships & cars. Catalog is in black & white, but the models, unless noted, are in full color.
Caribbean Kite Company	Quality stunt/sport kites & single-line kites for all ages.
Carla Corcini Exclusives	A fashionable collection of exclusive ready to wear wig designs for women with a huge selection of natural looking colors & special blends. Hairpieces, turbans, petal hats & wig accessories available at low mail order prices.
Cedco Collection	Calendars, books & CD-ROMs featuring top names
Celtic Highlight Catalog	Celtic imports & original items from Ireland, Scotland & Wales. Celebrate the Isles with our authentic range of music, jewelry, food, gifts & apparel

Catalog City is adding new catalogs & functionality all the time. This is intended to be a representation of the Catalog City Partner Store site. Please visit the Partner Store to see the current offerings.

Store	Type of Merchandise
Century Photo Products & Accessories	The broadest range of archival photographic storage, including photo pages, scrapbooks with acid-free paper, collectible supplies (stamps, postcards, sports cards) & CD/diskette storage.
Charlesbridge	Quality children's books that inform & fascinate. Topics included are counting & math, endangered species, outdoor adventures & multiculturalism.
Chef's Catalog	Professional restaurant equipment for the Home Chef, since 1979.
Cherry Tree	Plans, kits & supplies for wood-based projects, including clocks, bird feeders, toys, whirligigs, yard art, garden furniture & a large variety of special projects. There are projects available for a variety of tools & skill levels from novice to expert.
Cheryl & Co.	Cookie & gift assortments & gift baskets.
Children's Personalized Audio Cassette Tapes	Cassette tapes personalized with individual children's names. Theme selections include "My Birthday Tape", "Songs About Me", "My Christmas Tape", & "Disney Babies Personalized Lullabies".
Classic Cookbooks	Regional & non-regional cookbooks & cookbook software.
The Comfort Corner Clearance Corner	Women's footwear, comfort clothing & accessories in regular & hard-to-find sizes at clearance prices discounted up to 70%.
ComputerGear	Fun computer gifts for yourself, family, & friends! Lots of Star Wars, mouse pads, t-shirts, office décor, robots, kids' stuff, computer snacks, jewelry & more!
Comtrad Tech Update	Innovative products that represent the best technology from the world's premier manufacturers, including communication devices, health & wellness, & home products.

Catalog City is adding new catalogs & functionality all the time. This is intended to be a representation of the Catalog City Partner Store site. Please visit the Partner Store to see the current offerings.

Store	Type of Merchandise
Cook Brothers	A large selection of household & gift products, including jewelry, kitchen tools & cookware, electronics & toys.
Cook Brothers Sharp Side	A large selection of knives, self-defense & action gear, hardware & jewelry.
Cookie Bouquets	Floral-like arrangements using colored cellophane-wrapped chocolate chip cookies on stems. The products are delivered locally & shipped nationwide.
Cookie Island	Various types of cookies baked from scratch, including chocolate chip oats, white chocolate macadamia & peanut butter crunch. Cookies are available in gift boxes, gift tins and as mixes.
The Crafty Needle	Needlepoint, counted & stamped cross-stitch, paint by number, crochet, craft books, longstitch, crewel, latchhook & felt books on a variety of themes, including Jewish themes. Needlework supplies are also available.
Creations by Cranford	Quality, hand-crafted, solid furniture & home decorating accessories. Each item is offered in a variety of finishes, colors & styles with optional hand-painted designs.
Damart	Thermolactyl underwear & accessories providing lightweight warmth in many styles for men & women. With our underwear, you can choose the level of warmth best suited for you from one of our four grades.
Dancing Feathers Studio	Recycled-paper notecards, bookmarks & prints featuring original wildlife artwork.
Diamond Essence	Simulated diamond jewelry including pendants, bracelets, rings & watches.
Dick Blick Art Materials	Art materials & craft supplies including paints, canvas, modeling clay & drawing pens.

Catalog City is adding new catalogs & functionality all the time. This is intended to be a representation of the Catalog City Partner Store site. Please visit the Partner Store to see the current offerings.

Store	Type of Merchandise
Divali Candlelights Co.	Let Divali Candlelights Co. take you on a unique, global journey with the finest in candles & home accents.
Divers Direct	Brand name SCUBA & snorkel gear from AquaLung/US Divers, TUSA, MARES, Cochran, Tilos, Freestyle, Ikelite, UK, Princeton Tec & many others. Everything is always at a great price & always in stock, with an inventory of more than $3 million.
Dog Breed Products	Ties with an illustration of your favorite dog breed woven into the fabric.
Dogwise	A selection of more than 2000 dog training books & videos. It features the latest trends in training & behavior, natural health, clicker, showing, obedience, breeding, agility, veterinary & grooming.
Double Diamond Gloves	Western style Gauntlets & Fringed Gauntlets custom gloves
Dovetail Designs	Knitting & crochet patterns, books, kits & yarn packs designed by Val Love. Knit (by hand or machine) mini-dolls & animals, & sweaters for children & adults. Crochet patterns for nursery rhyme afghans, shoulder bags, backpacks, hats & crowns.
Drake World Band	Products for the short-wave enthusiast and amateur radio operator, including receivers, speakers, VHF converters & SW8 carrying cases.
Duncraft	Everything you need to attract wild birds to your backyard including feeders, houses, baths, seed, suet & nature related gifts.

Catalog City is adding new catalogs & functionality all the time. This is intended to be a representation of the Catalog City Partner Store site. Please visit the Partner Store to see the current offerings.

Store	Type of Merchandise
Dynamic Living	Solutions for easier living including kitchen appliances & household gadgets. Easy-to-use products for opening jars, cleaning up spills, changing channels on the TV, making telephone calls and many other daily living tasks.
The Eastwood Company	Unique automotive tools & supplies for the hobbyist & professional.
Easy Built Structures, Ltd.	Easy-to-assemble storage & recreation solutions for every lifestyle including storage buildings, barn style & gable designs, gazebos, spa enclosures, weekend cottage & playhouses.
Eco Enterprises – Hydroponics	Everything you need to start growing hydroponically, including Eco's own line of nutrients – manufactured for more than 26 years. Eco is a proven name in the world of hydroponics.
Educational Impressions	Instructional materials for teachers & educators of elementary & middle grade students. The catalog's line of workbooks encourages students to think & have fun while learning.
Ehrman Tapestry	A wide range of styles including traditional & contemporary patterns by famous textile artists Kaffe Fasset, Elian McCready, Margaret Murton, Candace Bahouth & many more. Perfect projects for the novice or expert stitcher.
EJ Gold's Earthenworks	Handpainted ceramics including vases, urns, bowls, plates & platters. All are available in three distinctive designs: City in the Sky, Woman in Red, and Dreaming Woman.
ElectroSensor EMF Detector	The Electro Sensor Electromagnetic Field Detector, used to measure the levels of EMF emitted by household appliances including clock radios, computers & microwaves.

Catalog City is adding new catalogs & functionality all the time. This is intended to be a representation of the Catalog City Partner Store site. Please visit the Partner Store to see the current offerings.

Store	Type of Merchandise
Elite Occasions Gift Baskets	Elegant gift baskets for every occasion. The gift baskets are perfect for guests or business partners.
English Country Signs	Individually designed & manufactured house signs & commercial signs. A combination of traditional styles & space age materials, our beautiful signs lend a touch of elegance & sophistication to your home or business.
English Faire Gifts	A variety of gifts made in Great Britain. These include personal wax seals, brass bookmarks, letter openers, paper knives, calligraphy supplies, paperweights & key rings.
English-Reading	Videos, workbooks & software for teachers of English & reading. These resource materials are geared toward middle & secondary classes.
Everything Wireless	Cutting-edge wireless products & services including cellular & PCS phones & other accessories.
Ex Officio	Multi-functional travel clothing designed for the active traveler.
Eximious of London	Gifts including jewelry, luggage, handbags & belts, picture frames & desk accessories.
Fabrics for the Home	Thousands of decorator fabrics for drapery & upholstery at mill direct prices saving you 30-70% over decorative jobber books.
Family Heirlooms	Personalized heraldry & heritage related products & giftware.
Favorite Homes	Sketches & simplified floor plans of homes whose blueprints are printed to order. Our designs are mostly traditional, with sizes from 800 – 5000 square feet. We can customize our designs as well.

Catalog City is adding new catalogs & functionality all the time. This is intended to be a representation of the Catalog City Partner Store site. Please visit the Partner Store to see the current offerings.

Store	Type of Merchandise
Femail Creations	Products to inspire women, including items for home & health as well as a variety of fun items for any occasion.
Festival	Twenty-three shades of Festival® brand colored & glitter hair sprays for salons, theatrical & clown uses, novelty or masquerade uses. There are also color & glitter gels for the hair as well as skin jewels for the skin.
Flavor Matters	All-natural professional cooking ingredients with no MSG including soup bases, sauce preps & flavor concentrates made for chefs & now available to home cooks.
Foot Traffic®	A wonderful collection of fun & novel fashions for legs & feet, including a wide variety of printed tights in sizes ranging from children's to queen. Also included are a large selection of toe socks, thigh highs, fishnet tights & fun slippers.
For Counsel, Inc.	Products & gifts for lawyers & other professionals. Included are products ranging from traditional to humorous. This catalog is a complete resource for legal gifts, furnishings & productivity tools.
From the Garden...To the Kitchen	Specialty books & products for the gardener who loves to cook & the cook who loves to garden. Products include garden & kitchen tools & accessories, cabinet knobs & pulls, cookbooks & gardening books for your home.
Frontgate	High quality products ranging from kitchen, bath & home office accessories to electronics & outdoor furniture.
Frontgate Gifts	Our annual collection of exceptional products for gift giving. This catalog is available only during the Fall/Holiday season.

Catalog City is adding new catalogs & functionality all the time. This is intended to be a representation of the Catalog City Partner Store site. Please visit the Partner Store to see the current offerings.

Store	Type of Merchandise
FultonStreet.com	A taste of New York's Famous Fulton Fish Market "Delivered from the ocean to your home" anywhere in the USA! The fish truck has been replaced by the toll-free phone, the Internet, the credit card & UPS guaranteeing fresh next day delivery. Complimentary recipes with every purchase (by star chef Nick Morfogen) create a truly unique & enjoyable package.
A Gentle Wind	Award-winning children's recordings, music & storytelling for infants through age eight.
George Scatchard Lamps	Table lamps & floor lamps in many styles & colors. The lamps are handmade in Vermont and sold nationally.
Glass Cartoons® by Carl Goeller	Personalized glass figures in designs representing every occupation, event or celebration, including medical & service people, educators, sports, weddings & retirement scenes. Glass figures are available as collectibles, cardholders, trophies, executive gifts & promotional items.
Golden Valley Lighting	Lighting fixtures including lamps & chandeliers.
Good Catalog	The best of all possible worlds, including home & family products, seasonal gifts & décor, collectibles, premier outdoor entertaining & garden items, exceptional jewelry, kids' products & much more.
Graftobian – Clown Noses	Hand-crafted clown noses that are very light, feel real, are very soft & comfortably conform to the contour of your own nose. These noses come in many shapes & sizes. They are available in bright red, flesh tone, glitter, pearlized pink & pearlized purple.

Store	Type of Merchandise
Graftobian Limited	Disguise Stix® makeup that is easy to use, non-toxic, temporary coloring for skin & hair. Removed with soap & water, each Disguise Stix® provides enough coloring to cover the average face several times.
Graftobian Theatrical	A full line of professional theatrical makeup for stage & screen. We have individual makeup & accessories along with kits & palettes for professional character makeup application.
Grand Era	Victorian & country style reproductions for outdoor home décor & furniture including decorative porch brackets, porch posts, railings, gable end decorations, gates, mail box posts, porch swings & custom reproductions.
grandparent's toy connection	Classic & creative toys for grandkids or any kids, including nostalgic toys as well as gifts for grandparents.
Gravity Plus	Backcare products including inversion therapy exercise equipment & ergonomic seating.
The Great Gift Source	A unique source of exciting gift ideas for everyone on your list. Our collection includes decorative accessories for the home, dolls, children's products, keepsake books, journals, stationery & jewelry. Also included are calligraphy prints with meaningful verses. Most items can be elegantly gift wrapped for the perfect finishing touch.
H.S. Trask & Co.	A collection of H.S. Trask footwear for men. H.S. Trask footwear is hand-crafted in the USA using America's original leathers, including elk, longhorn & bison. They combine superior leathers with the finest construction methods to make shoes that are comfortable right out of the box.

Catalog City is adding new catalogs & functionality all the time. This is intended to be a representation of the Catalog City Partner Store site. Please visit the Partner Store to see the current offerings.

Store	Type of Merchandise
Hagensborg Foods	Gourmet foods including seafood, chocolate, confections, olive oil, Spanish products, pate, butter toffee, salmon & specialty foods.
Hammacher Schlemmer	Hammacher's first toy collection with innovative gifts for your kids.
Hammond Groves	Deliciously memorable Holiday gifts of oranges & grapefruit from Florida's renowned Indian River Citrus Region.
Healthware 2	Exceptional pillows & other handmade tools for relaxing & stress relief, including eye pillows, buckwheat hull pillows & thermal pillows. Pillows are made with exquisite silk & cotton fabrics & organic fillings & are useful for home, office & traveling.
HearthSong	Unique toys, arts & crafts, games, puzzles, dolls & books for parents looking for healthy, educational gifts for children.
Heavenly Treasures	Exquisite & fine jewelry for women including unique & hard-to-find items at excellent prices.
The Herbfarm	Unique herbal products to heal, help with sleep, sharpen one's mind, ease a cold, brighten one's mood, amuse a pet & flavor one's food.
Higher Octave Music	Music from smooth jazz to new age, ambient to world beat & rock oriented to symphonic orchestrations. The merchandise includes artists 3rd force, Craig Chaquico, Near Schon, Ottmar Liebert, Cusco, Grant Graissman & Jon Anderson.
Holiday Works Select Series	Assembled, pre-lit & pre-decorated Christmas trees which are delivered ready to roll into place & plug-in. Choose from eight designs. Matching wreaths, garlands & accessories are also available to complete your holiday décor.

Catalog City is adding new catalogs & functionality all the time. This is intended to be a representation of the Catalog City Partner Store site. Please visit the Partner Store to see the current offerings.

Store	Type of Merchandise
The Home Marketplace	Clever items for the kitchen & the home including products for entertaining, cooking, organizing & cleaning. There is an innovative product for every room in your household.
Home Visions	Decorating trends for your home featuring fashion bedding products, decorative furniture & accent accessories as well as seasonal products for the home.
The HomeStyles® Collection	The latest collection of home design products from HomeStyles. Home design software & books from HomeStyles give you access to the world's largest collection of residential home designs – over 10,000. All homes are designed by AIA or AIBD-certified designers; complete construction drawings are available for every design.
Hoop House Greenhouse Kits	Greenhouse kits, available in 11 standard sizes. Hoop house greenhouses can be used for plants, as aviaries & chicken coops, dry storage of kindling & firewood, or even as temporary home additions, including garages & breezeways.
Horchow	Home furnishings, accessories & decorative items
Hydrokinetic – Body Friendly	A unique line of aquatic exercise, water sports & pool game products that enhance health, strength, endurance & the enjoyment of life. The products include a water running floatation belt, Hydrokinetic bells, pool footwear & pool games.
IBIS Catalog Co.	Unique handcrafted ethnic gifts, home accents & fashion accessories, including an eclectic selection of candles, candleholders, African carvings, ancient Egyptian art, bodycare products & other timeless treasures.

Catalog City is adding new catalogs & functionality all the time. This is intended to be a representation of the Catalog City Partner Store site. Please visit the Partner Store to see the current offerings.

Store	Type of Merchandise
Idaho Wood	Contemporary lighting fixtures made of cedar or oak for interior or exterior use. Styles include post, wall, ceiling, street, valence & strip lights.
iGO	Mobile computing accessories from model-specific accessories to wireless devices. Providing solutions for people on the go with enough gear to completely outfit over 20,000 models of cell phones & laptop computers.
Illuminations	The largest selection of fine quality candles. Hand poured, and in most cases handmade, we make & formulate our candles with superior quality ingredients. Our candleholders & other accessories are equally unique & cannot be found anywhere else.
Improved Living	The latest trends in health care, including vitamin & herbal supplements, homeopathic remedies, magnetics, traditional beauty aids, self-care products & a large assortment of items to make everyday chores easier.
Indian Harvest	Premium rice, grains & beans as well as taste-tempting gift assortments & serving accessories. Everything you need to make incredibly healthy & delicious meals.
Indonesian Elements	An eclectic collection of sterling silver jewelry & collectible art imported from Indonesia, including a variety of gift items such as amber jewelry, sun boxes & tribal, masks from Bali.
Internatural	Natural products that promote wellness & conscious living.

Store	Type of Merchandise
investorsoftware.com	Financial analysis software to understand your company's true financial performance or determine its worth. Detailed technical analysis to chart, screen & filter stocks that outperform the competition. Other topics include real estate & capital raising.
Isabella Bird	Beautiful, quality clothing that is made for women. Isabella Bird clothing celebrates adventure, travel, life & literature. The clothing is stylish, sophisticated, comfortable & can be found no where else.
Isla	Great gifts for the Holidays, this issue highlights Christmas music & cards, books, videos, gourmet coffees & lots of new craft gift items from Puerto Rico, Cuba & their Caribbean neighbors.
J. Jill	Women's apparel, natural fiber sportswear, shoes & accessories.
Jade Mountain	A comprehensive selection (more than 5000 products) of sustainable products & renewable energy systems, including worldwide supply, design, sizing, installations & trouble-shooting of solar electric, micro-hydro, wind generators, composting toilets, greywater systems & super energy efficient appliances.
Jamestown Distributors	General supplies & equipment for woodworking, boat building & construction products, including innovative tool tips & techniques. This catalog also offers weatherproof stainless steel, silicon bronze & brass screws, nail bolts, nuts, washers & hardware.

Catalog City is adding new catalogs & functionality all the time. This is intended to be a representation of the Catalog City Partner Store site. Please visit the Partner Store to see the current offerings.

Store	Type of Merchandise
Japan Woodworker Catalog of Fine Woodworking Tools	Japanese laminated chisels & plane blades, water stones, razor saws garden tools & cutlery. Woodworking tools are from a wide variety of Japanese, European & American toolmakers (such as L.S. Starrett).
Joan Cook	A potpourri of items encompassing housewares, kitchen items, home furnishings, gifts, apparel, personal items & novelties.
Jollys Garden Shoes	Injection molded garden & leisure-time shoes & clogs with orthopedically designed removable cotton covered molded natural cork "footbed" insoles.
jumpmusic.com	The world's best music software, more than 5 million pages of sheet music, tablature, electronic piano keyboards & music accessories.
Just My Size	Famous brand-name plus sizes from Just My Size, Hanes, Playtex, Body Language, Bali, Glamorise, Champion Woman, Hanes Signature & more.
Key West Conch Traders	Over 450 unique items from Key West, Florida, including art, collectibles & specialty items.
Kid Territory	Ideas & products to help create fun, learning environments for kids aged 2 to 11. This catalog is full of original products, including cozy reading furniture, wall decorations kids can play with and unique displays for showing off kids' artwork & collections.
Knapp Boots & Shoes	Designed Knapp footwear including the famous Two-Shot™ shock absorbing work shoes & boots, tested best Grabbers™ slip resistant footwear & ANSI approved steel toe boot & shoes.

Catalog City is adding new catalogs & functionality all the time. This is intended to be a representation of the Catalog City Partner Store site. Please visit the Partner Store to see the current offerings.

Store	Type of Merchandise
Lane Bryant	The largest selection of fashions for women's sizes 14 to 60 including dresses, sportswear, coats, intimates & footwear. The merchandise is available in women's, women's petite, misses, tall & half sizes.
Lagenbach Fine Garden Tools	Fine garden tools & equipment for the avid gardener. Also included are decorative accents, including pottery, planters, arbors, trellises, statues, fountains & garden benches.
Laser Labels	Top quality labels for inkjet & laser printers. The catalog also includes self-adhesive labels for all types of computer-controlled printers.
Leslie Dame Enterprises, Ltd.	Multi-media, compact disc, audiocassette, videocassette, DVD storage cabinets & racks. We offer a wide variety of sizes & finishes in an assortment of woods. We also have large capacity storage systems for collections of all sizes.
Leslie Levy Fine Art, Inc.	Fine art posters & lithographs, serigraphs & limited editions by 55 outstanding artists known for their landscapes, wildlife, florals, figurative, gardenscapes, photography & Southwestern imagery. Popular artists include Steve Hanks, Terry Isaac, Kent Wallis & Raymond I. Knaub.
The Lighthouse Catalog	Products designed to make life easier for people with impaired vision — at home, in the workplace & at play. Catalogs are available in large print, Braille, cassette & disk formats.
Lighthouse Depot	The most complete selection of lighthouse memorabilia ever assembled, including books, distinctive lighting, jewelry, videos, prints & replicas. Also featured are the complete Harbour Lights collectibles & Spencer Collin Collections.

Catalog City is adding new catalogs & functionality all the time. This is intended to be a representation of the Catalog City Partner Store site. Please visit the Partner Store to see the current offerings.

Store	Type of Merchandise
Lilliput	An extensive collection of fine quality tin mechanical wind-up toys, scale model vehicles, vintage clocks & die cast vehicles. Most items are limited editions & are of European origin.
Linen Source	Linens including bedding & window treatments.
Lone Wolf	Unique, hand-made, individually painted items that capture the Southwestern tradition, including painted feathers, dream catchers, pottery geckos & turtles, miniature kokopellis, bears & buffalo. Also featured are bird & hummingbird feeders.
Magnolia Hall	More than 300 Victorian furnishings & accessories, many of which are not available elsewhere. The merchandise includes tufted sofas & marble-top tables for the living room, hand-carved four-posters & dressers, lamps & mirrors.
Martial Arts Supplies by I & I Sports	Training equipment, martial arts weapons & uniforms, books & videos for the martial artist specializing in Filipino Martial Arts, Jeet Kune Do or Pro Boxing.
Mauna Loa	Gourmet food & other specialties of the Hawaiian Islands, including macadamia nuts, assorted candy & chocolates, hibiscus plants, fresh orchid lei, rich Kona coffee & other delectable treats.
Maus & Hoffman	Men's & women's quality, ready-to-wear clothing with a Florida flair.
Michigan Bicycle Touring	A wide variety of weekend & weeklong vacation packages for active people. Highlighting these trips is the spectacular beauty of northern Michigan.
Miller Stockman Western Wear	Western wear for men & women including hats, coats, boots & dresses.

Catalog City is adding new catalogs & functionality all the time. This is intended to be a representation of the Catalog City Partner Store site. Please visit the Partner Store to see the current offerings.

Store	Type of Merchandise
Ministry of the Arts	Unique gifts with an inspirational message, including calendars, prints, cards, music & sculpture.
Modern Farm	Country lifestyle products, including handy household items, apparel, gardening accessories, tools, auto accessories & farm supplies.
Mrs. Beasley's Miss Grace Lemon Cakes	Cakes, muffins, cookies & other desserts presented in a way that will draw "oohs" & "ahs" from your gift recipients.
Mrs. Fields Gourmet Gifts	A wide variety of gift packages for all of your gift-giving occasions filled with Mrs. Fields fresh-baked treats.
Multicultural Textiles	Handcrafted home & fashion accessories from East & West Africa & Guatemala, including handcrafted bedding, plates, candleholders, pillows, napkin rings & bookends.
Museum Tour	Museum quality educational toys, games, gifts & kits for children, teachers & adults. Includes science, art, robotics, crafts, CDs, musical instruments, jewelry & sculpture.
Musicmaker's	Materials for building your own musical instrument. The catalog also includes blueprints, kits & books for harps, dulcimers, stands, lute, hurdy gurdy & guitars.
My Grandma's	Gourmet, kosher, coffee cakes, gifts, gift baskets & corporate gifts. Cake flavors include : Cinnamon Walnut, Granny Smith apple, Cappuccino, Golden Raspberry, New England Blueberry & Banana Walnut. Low fat cakes are also available.

Catalog City is adding new catalogs & functionality all the time. This is intended to be a representation of the Catalog City Partner Store site. Please visit the Partner Store to see the current offerings.

Store	Type of Merchandise
Name Than Toon	Original animation & advertising artworks used in the most popular television commercials from America's most famous corporations. Also featured in the catalog are advertising, plush bears & celebrity rubber ducks.
Natasha's Café & Boutique	Turkish & Greek coffee, art, artifacts & fashion from around the world. Products reflect the atmosphere of Natasha's Café & Boutique (a real place), where you can ask the dishwasher the meaning of life, copy the recipes off the menu, discuss & chat. A store definitely too weird to franchise.
National Geographic Society	All the tools you need to carry out your own explorations: travel gear & clothing field tested by Geographic staff, National Geographic maps, books, CD-ROMs, scientific instruments of the highest quality & collectible objects that reflect the unique origins of their cultures.
Naturally Northwest	Delicious gourmet foods from the beautiful Pacific Northwest. Try regional favorites including coffee, chocolate, sauces, jams, meats, cooking oils, spices, gift baskets & more.
Nelson Candle & Beeswax	Handcrafted beeswax candles scented with natural fragrances for elegance, aromatherapy, passion & romance.
Northwest River Supplies — Paddlesports Equipment Guide	Rafts, kayaks, canoes, cars & paddles, camping equipment, apparel & accessories.
Northwest's Best	The finest handcrafted functional art pieces from the Pacific Northwest. Products include home decorating items, jewelry, value added wood products, pottery, furniture, bedding, garden accessories & natural forest products.

Catalog City is adding new catalogs & functionality all the time. This is intended to be a representation of the Catalog City Partner Store site. Please visit the Partner Store to see the current offerings.

Store	Type of Merchandise
Novagraphics Space Art	Realistic & accurate art of the cosmos by top artists from books, magazines, TV & movies. Items include originals, prints, posters & cards.
Okun Brothers Shoes	Quality brand name shoes offered in many sizes & widths at discount prices, including New Balance, Hush Puppies, Clarks, Rockport, Mephisto, Bostonian, Soft Spots, Reiker, Sebago, Footjoy & Haflinger. Extra-large or extra-wide sizes are available in most items.
Old Frontier Clothing Co.	Authentic Western-style & Victorian influenced Western clothing for men & women, including hats, pants, shirts, vests & leather goods.
The Old Time Signery	Fine reproductions of "old" wooden signs & plaques. Many feature personalization. Categories include: golf, trades, medical, financial, business, hobbies, Irish, wildlife, billiards, humorous, functional signs and many more!
One Hanes Place	Famous brands of hosiery, intimates & casualwear at great savings, including Hanes®, L'eggs®, Just My Size®, Wonderbra®, Bali® & Playtex®. Also included is exclusive Hanes Signature® Casualwear.
One Island	The finest collection of island gifts & treasures, including Aloha shirts, gourmet foods, books, music, jewelry & art.
Orchid Select	Arrangements of cut flowers & live orchid plants direct from our greenhouse. When the occasion calls for something truly special, orchids capture the moment for birthdays, anniversaries, housewarmings or that romantic gift. Containers & accessories are also available for that special gift.

Catalog City is adding new catalogs & functionality all the time. This is intended to be a representation of the Catalog City Partner Store site. Please visit the Partner Store to see the current offerings.

Store	Type of Merchandise
Oriental Trading	Treats, toys, novelties & giftware for children of all ages, including pencils, keychains, party decorations, giftwrap & party favors.
Orientalia	Oriental figures, wall hangings, jewelry, snuff bottles & netsuke. Figurines are made of such materials as ivory, bone, wood, glass, cloisonné, jade & semi-precious stones.
The Pack Basket: A Mountain Classics Catalog	A collection of mountain classics for the home including rustic furniture & accessories, casual clothing, jewelry & gifts.
Paintball Guns & Accessories by I & I Sports	The most extensive line of guns, accessories, safety equipment & apparel for the sport of paintball.
Panache, For Those Who Love to Entertain	A fine selection of products supporting the home entertaining experience, including tabletop, home décor, social items, gifts & furniture.
Paper Goodies from Judy's Place	MagiCloth toys & dolls featuring the art of Judy M. Johnson. Catalog also includes commercial limited-edition paper dolls signed by the artist.
The Parks Company	The first & only National Park Catalog offering the greatest collection of National Park themed products anywhere. A spectacular collection of National Park art, apparel, gifts, limited edition collectibles, home accessories books, multimedia & more. The only catalog completely dedicated to celebrating & supporting America's National Parks with a donation to the parks made from every item sold.
Pentagonia	Quality outdoor clothing & gear for climbing, skiing, hiking & more.

Catalog City is adding new catalogs & functionality all the time. This is intended to be a representation of the Catalog City Partner Store site. Please visit the Partner Store to see the current offerings.

Store	Type of Merchandise
Patterncrafts	Craft patterns from more than 150 pattern designers & publishers. We offer a variety of patterns for fabric, felt & wood crafts, continually updating our selection with new patterns to keep you current with the latest craft trends & ideas.
Peak Ski & Sport Lifestyles	Gear, gifts, jewelry & accessories for the active outdoor lifestyle, such as skiing & snowboarding.
Pendleton Cowgirl Company	Captivating, turn-of-the-century photo-art prints of pioneer cowgirls who competed in rodeos throughout the country from 1910 to 1930. The collection features seven high-quality prints & one 36-by-36-inch handpainted silk scarf.
Penn Street Bakery	Specialty cakes baked from scratch "like a marriage of cheesecake & poundcake" & garnished with fresh fruits, powdered sugar, sauces or decorative icing.
Personal Creations	Personalized gifts for holidays & special occasions. Personal Creations can create a unique keepsake for you or anyone on your gift-giving list. These gifts are perfect for weddings, baptisms, new babies, graduations & special people in your life.
The Personal Touch	Unique items personalized with your name & address. Choose from personalized self-stick name & address labels, self-inking name & address stamps, stationery, pencils, business cards, luggage tags, gifts, children's items & much more.
PestChaser Electronic Rodent Repeller	Electronic rodent repellers in tabletop & plug-in models for kitchen, garages, vacation homes & anywhere else rodents may hide.

Catalog City is adding new catalogs & functionality all the time. This is intended to be a representation of the Catalog City Partner Store site. Please visit the Partner Store to see the current offerings.

Store	Type of Merchandise
Pet Bird Xpress Birdalog	Unique & extraordinary products for pet birds & their humans, including books, toys, bird harnesses, cleaning supplies, videos, feeders, water bottles, speech & trick training, gifts, Hagen Tropican, Roudybush, Lafeber, Vitalites & much more!
Peters Feeders	Bird feeding equipment & supplies for hummingbirds, orioles, finches & cardinals.
Plow & Hearth	Outdoor furnishings, gardening tools & products for country living.
The Popcorn Factory	Gourmet popcorn & other treats beautifully presented in gift baskets, tins & packages.
The Port Canvas Company	Manufactured in Kennebunkport, Maine. Fine quality, durable canvas duffels, tote bags, soft luggage, handbags, ski & boot bags, belts, keychains, dog leashes & accessories. Choice of 12 canvas colors & three trim colors. Monogramming available.
Porter Case Luggage With Cart	A patented, U.S. made, hard-side carry-on size wheeled luggage case with a built-in cart. It weighs less than 12 pounds yet will carry 200 pounds on top when converted into a cart. The case has four-inch ball-bearing wheels, a combination lock & a padded 42-inch extension handle.
Porto Banus	Effortless women's fashions with a spirit of adventure. Shopping takes on a new meaning as leisure fashions move in harmony with Annie's world-wide travels aboard her sailing vessel...Porto Banus.

Catalog City is adding new catalogs & functionality all the time. This is intended to be a representation of the Catalog City Partner Store site. Please visit the Partner Store to see the current offerings.

Store	Type of Merchandise
Precision Auto Designs	Fine quality & value in accessories for Mercedes-Benz vehicle owners, including commuting comforts, performance enhancers, restoration & maintenance parts.
Price Cutter	Value-priced router bits & woodworking accessories.
Priorities – Allergy Relief & a Healthy Home	High quality medically tested environmental control products for allergies & asthma. These products are all proven effective in protecting you from allergens, asthma triggers & chemical toxins.
Proline	Accessories for the home entertainment & computer environment, including audio, video, computer care & storage products.
Protective Wear — Safety Wear	Raincoats, rainsuits, boots & ponchos in several qualities & colors. Products are available for industrial & home consumer use. Industrial coveralls are also available.
Puerta Bella.com	Eclectic home décor & gifts reflecting the colors of Spain, warmth of Mexico, spices of India & style of Italy. All selections are handmade from solid wood, forged iron, vibrant glass & pottery. Free shipping & fast delivery.
Putnam Rolling Ladders	Rolling ladders made of the best grade red oak & designed with the grace & beauty of fine furniture. These ladders are available in various wood finishes & are great for homes, libraries & offices. Also featured are step stools, rolling platform ladders & "top bent" rolling ladders for lofts

Catalog City is adding new catalogs & functionality all the time. This is intended to be a representation of the Catalog City Partner Store site. Please visit the Partner Store to see the current offerings.

Store	Type of Merchandise
R'Tish Umoja	Custom & individually hand-crafted items ranging from imported Egyptian reproductions & leather-crafts to artifacts from African countries such as Kenya & Nigeria. The catalog features collectible quality handcrafted dolls, pecan shell resins, linens, professional golf apparel, custom imported mahogany furniture, inspirational books & tapes.
RACELINE DIRECT	Classic NASCAR polo shirts, driver uniform jackets, racing gear & gift items.
RailRiders: Adventure Clothing	Adventure clothing for the adventure-seeking lifestyle. This catalog includes lightweight & stylish technical apparel for active travelers, camping enthusiasts, hikers & multisport athletes.
Raven Maps & Images	A collection of United States, world & special interest maps. These are more than geography...they're art.
Real Cookies	Gourmet cookie mixes including shortbread & sugar cookies. Tins of fresh-baked cookies, fortune cookies, decorated Oreos & pizza cookies.
Real Goods Catalog	Products for sustainable & healthy living. Real Goods is the pioneer in air & water purification, energy-efficient lighting, non-toxic cleaning, natural pest control, solar powered lighting & recycling products for the home. Everything you need for the environmental home.
Rediscover Music Catalogue	Hard-to-find CDs from the "folk era" (1957-1967), including those by Peter, Paul & Mary, the Kingston Trio, the Chad Mitchell Trio & the Limeliters. Also included is music from Bob Dylan & the Seekers, cowboy music & bluegrass, Celtic & comedy albums.

Catalog City is adding new catalogs & functionality all the time. This is intended to be a representation of the Catalog City Partner Store site. Please visit the Partner Store to see the current offerings.

Store	Type of Merchandise
Remarkable Products	Your business-to-business solution for corporate calendars, maps, planners, motivational posters, office supplies & more.
Rent Mother Nature	"A farmer's market by mail." All Rent Mother Nature plans start with a calligraphied & personalized Lease Document for the crop of your choice.
Rhythm Band Instruments	Plenty of quality rhythmic & melodic instruments make music fun for all ages. Now the whole family can "play" together on many levels – from basic rhythm kits to recorder ensemble playing. Music can enhance & make our lives richer.
Rocke's Meating Haus	CERTIFIED ANGUS BEEF™ steaks & other specialty & smoked meats. For over 60 years we've applied the Rocke family craft to the art of smoked meats. Still using only hardwood hickory & our slow delicate smoking process, our hams are smoked for over 24 hours for an amazingly rich smoked flavor & tenderness. Our CERTIFIED ANGUS BEEF™ steaks & roasts are aged to perfection, carefully selected & hand-cut for the ultimate in tenderness & flavor.
Rockler Woodworking and Hardware	Hard to find hardware, wood, tools & supplies for woodworkers, do it yourselfers, furniture restorers, cabinet makers & crafters. Great tools & jigs for your shop, innovative furniture & cabinet hardware, exotic hardwoods & veneers.
Rod's Western Palace	A complete selection of Western lifestyle clothing, including boots, hats, jeans, shirts & gifts.
Ross-Simons	Fine jewelry, famous name tableware, collectibles, gifts & furniture.

Catalog City is adding new catalogs & functionality all the time. This is intended to be a representation of the Catalog City Partner Store site. Please visit the Partner Store to see the current offerings.

Store	Type of Merchandise
The Rubberstampler	Thousands of stamp designs for all seasons & reasons, including exclusive designs to decorate greeting cards, stationery, invitations & fabric, plus custom stamps, accessories, stickers, stencils & paper. This catalog has everything you need for your stamping pleasure!
SalsaExpress	Spicy Southwestern foods including gourmet salsas, chips, peppers & hot snacks. Selections include hot & spicy "Scovie" & "Premium Choices". Also available are great gift items & T-shirts.
San Francisco Music Box & Gift Company	Gifts, collectibles & musical jewelry boxes of all kinds.
Santa Barbara Olive Co., Inc.	Seasonings & condiments, specializes in handpicked olives, olive oil, Geno's garlic nectar & other condiments.
Schnee's Boots & Shoes	Quality outdoor footwear & clothing. Whether for trips into the wilderness or just running errands when it's snowing or raining, Schnee's has the gear you need.
SeasonScape.com	Great holiday candles & accessories!
Sensational Beginnings	Provides us with toys & tools that celebrate the wonders of childhood.
The Sharper Image	Innovative products to enhance every aspect of your life. The product line includes stereos, personal care items, note recorders, radios, walkie-talkies, cameras & products available exclusively through The Sharper Image.
Simpson & Vail	More than 130 types of bulk teas, from black to oolongs & greens to flavored & herbal. Also included are teapots, teacups, tea paraphernalia, 50 types of coffee & an assortment of gourmet specialty food items.

Catalog City is adding new catalogs & functionality all the time. This is intended to be a representation of the Catalog City Partner Store site. Please visit the Partner Store to see the current offerings.

Store	Type of Merchandise
Smith-Victor Lighting & Accessories	Photography & video lighting equipment including light meters, lighting kits, stands & accessories.
Smucker's Catalog	Smucker's famous preserves, jams, jellies, syrup toppings & natural peanut butters, plus gifts & accents for the home that meet the Smucker's standard for high quality. You can even create unique gift assortments from the more than 100 flavors of jams, preserves, jellies & fruit butters. With a name like Smucker's, it has to be good.™
Solar Tan Thru Suits by Lifestyles Direct	Tan Thru swimwear that is so revolutionary, it's patented! Soft, comfortable microfibers allow suits to breathe & dry quickly. Lots of great designs, guaranteed to be tan-thru — not see thru — wet or dry!
The Soldier Factory	Original pewter chess sets handsculpted by professional craftsmen & artists. Sets include King Arthur, Richard the Lion Hearted, Civil War & many more.
Solo Sewing Supplies	A full line of sewing supplies serving the needs of cleaners, tailors, & bridal shops. Also offered are buttons, scissors, spotting guns, pressing machines, steamers, ironing boards, irons, coat hangers, poly bags, instruction books & videos.
Songbooks Unlimited	Songbooks & musical self-improvement methods for keyboard, pop, jazz, classical & sacred music.
Sorice Asana Systems	High quality, attractive rack systems for stereo & video components & other home uses.

Catalog City is adding new catalogs & functionality all the time. This is intended to be a representation of the Catalog City Partner Store site. Please visit the Partner Store to see the current offerings.

Store	Type of Merchandise
Spaceshots – Images and Imagination	Posters & educational charts of satellite images from around the world, including many of the latest NASA photographs. Mugs, videos, CD-ROMs & gift cards are also available.
Spiratone	Photographic accessories for the professional & advanced amateur photographer, including studio lighting, backgrounds, portable power packs, filter systems & processors.
Sportif	Sport, resort & active wear & the trusted Sportif stretch sportswear.
Stacks & Stacks	Products for the home to help you store & organize, including computer stands & desks, tie racks, shower totes, closet organizers, entertainment storage systems & toy stacking carts.
Stafford's	Unique selection of apparel & gifts relating to hunting, dogs & being outdoors.
Stark & Legum Catalog	Hats For All Seasons: Fine quality & service of men's brand name hats & caps such as Stetson, Kangol, Dobbs, Biltmore, Akubra & a great deal more. Established 1924.
Steps	Classic, well made clothing for children ages 2-14.
Sunshine Jewelry	Fine jewelry at discount prices on today's most popular styles of glamorous, classic & casual jewelry. Included are earrings, bangles, chains, rings & bracelets; all at a savings of 67% or more.
SuperEar Personal Sound Enhancer	An electronic sound amplifier for use indoors & outdoors. It's great for bird watchers, sports enthusiasts & nature lovers.

Catalog City is adding new catalogs & functionality all the time. This is intended to be a representation of the Catalog City Partner Store site. Please visit the Partner Store to see the current offerings.

Store	Type of Merchandise
Sure Fit Slipcovers by Mail	Ready-made slipcovers in beautiful, machine washable fabrics. One-piece elasticized covers fit most upholstered furniture. Slipcovers allow you to cover old furniture, protect new furniture, or redecorate with ease.
Talbots Kids	Comfortable, durable & easy-to-wear clothes for boys & girls. Available in sizes 3-24 months for babies & sizes 2-16 for toddlers & older children.
The Territory Ahead	Upscale quality clothing that is durable, rugged & outdoorsy. Our unique clothing is designed & developed by us, using special fabrics & distinguishing details found nowhere else.
Terry's Village	Gifts & decorative accents for your home & garden in a style of country warmth & playful charm, all at affordable prices.
Thundering Herd Buffalo Products	Anything you can imagine made of buffalo. Products include buffalo skins, buffalo robes, buffalo leather, mounted heads & decorator skulls.
Timberline Archery Products	Archery accessories, including sight, Teflon cable slides & the highly acclaimed no-peep.
Time Well Spent	A wide range of items for gardening, outdoors, travel, fitness, golf, writing, art, music, family & gifts.
Timeke Funktional Kidswear	A Canadian children's wear line of brightly colored, prewashed, 100% cotton basics which coordinate beautifully with a seasonal line of cotton prints for ages 0 thru 10. Fun accessories, cozy sleepwear, plus bedding & more.

Catalog City is adding new catalogs & functionality all the time. This is intended to be a representation of the Catalog City Partner Store site. Please visit the Partner Store to see the current offerings.

Store	Type of Merchandise
Today's Kitchen	Functional & whimsical items for your kitchen, including cookware, tabletop, & kitchen textiles. Also contains a complete selection of kitchen electrics, including coffeemakers, toasters, microwave ovens, mixers & can openers by national brands, including Cuisinart, KitchenAid Fiestaware & T-Fal.
TopiX	Innovative items & electronics for home, office & leisure. Items include digital cameras, cordless phones, radio controlled vehicles & portable electronics such as TVs & DVD players.
The Trademark Collection	Merchandise exhibiting the world's most famous trademarks. The Trademark Collection is your number one source for collectibles, including die cast vehicles, porcelain boxes, cookie jars, salt & pepper shakers, ornaments, bears & dolls.
Travel 2000	Luggage & travel accessories for the business & recreational traveler including briefcases & computer cases with & without wheels for today's busy executive.
Travel Tools	Travel Tools for the business traveler. Everything you need to travel successfully for business is in this catalog. Included are the computer backpack, attaché cases, luggage, water-fillable weights & a currency converter.
TravelSmith Outfitting Guide and Catalog	Travel apparel, outdoor clothing, luggage & travel accessories for men & women. Tested everywhere from the Amazon to Annapurna, TravelSmith products are designed to withstand the rigors of the road.
Turn Off the TV	Family games, activities & educational toys to bring families & friends together.

Catalog City is adding new catalogs & functionality all the time. This is intended to be a representation of the Catalog City Partner Store site. Please visit the Partner Store to see the current offerings.

Store	Type of Merchandise
Twinkling Christmas Tree	Twinkling electronic Christmas trees, available with or without a scrolling message.
Unicorn Studios	Hard-to-find crafts & musical parts.
Universal Map Consumer Products Catalog	An extensive array of travel references, including North American road atlases, business & educational references, wall maps & children's travel activities.
Velo	Products that inspire, educate & entertain cycling enthusiasts & endurance athletes, including helpful training tools, sports history, T-shirts & accessories. This catalog has everything you need to demonstrate your enthusiasm for mountain biking, cycling, or multi-sport events.
Victorian Lampshades Supply Catalog	Victorian lampshades & the silk fabrics, bead fringes & other trims to make them. Reproduction lamps are also offered, along with easy-to-follow videos to help you restore, make or trim lampshades.
Victorian Trading Company	Victorian treasures, including lace, framed prints, stationery, jewelry, & home decorating items.
Virginia Born & Bred	Gifts reflecting Virginia's heritage with an emphasis on quality, uniqueness, tradition & craftsmanship. Items in the catalog include handmade jewelry, folk art pottery, food gift baskets & Civil War memorabilia.
Wanda's Nature Farm Foods	All natural & organically grown grains in delivery mixes for bread machines & conventional ovens. Also included are food storage items for bread & other bakery goods, including The Bread Box & The See-It-All Bread Box.
Water Me Frog	An electronic watering reminder for potted plants. The frog softly beeps & its eye blinks when your plant is thirsty.

Catalog City is adding new catalogs & functionality all the time. This is intended to be a representation of the Catalog City Partner Store site. Please visit the Partner Store to see the current offerings.

Store	Type of Merchandise
Wedding Ring Boutique	The finest in 14-carat, 18-karat & platinum wedding rings, bridal party gifts & special treasures for your wedding day.
West-Tex Collectibles	High-quality, limited edition die-cast collectibles, including Texaco, Coca-Cola & other major company logos. Also featured are a large selection of tin & porcelain signs, die-cast & wooden aircraft models.
What on Earth	A collection of fun wear & delightful diversions. This catalog offers whimsical gifts & collectibles. Our specialty is our exclusive tee-shirts & sweatshirts in many themes to suit every member of the family.
Whimsies by Bodoh & Henke	Whimsical sculptures handcrafted of solid copper & brass from the Key West, Florida, studio of Larry Henke & Ron Bodoh. Recycled metals are used when available; they will gain a rich natural patina with age & weather.
Wild Bird Mart	Specializing in bird feeders, bird houses & backyard accessories.
Wilderness Adventures	Books & videos on such subjects as bird hunting, fly fishing, fly tying & big game hunting, as well as cookbooks.
Wildlife Works	Men & women's organic cotton casual clothing. Our high quality range includes khaki's, polos, rib knits & our signature Safari Jacket. Proceeds support Wildlife Works unique wildlife conservation activities in Africa.
Wind in the Rigging	A selection of nautical gifts for your home, boat & office, including boating gear & accessories, nautical art, literature & sea chanteys & a collection of unique nautical jewelry & clothing.

Catalog City is adding new catalogs & functionality all the time. This is intended to be a representation of the Catalog City Partner Store site. Please visit the Partner Store to see the current offerings.

Store	Type of Merchandise
Winona	Sweaters, sportswear & unique gifts. Comfort, quality & satisfaction are guaranteed.
The Women's Golf Catalog	Thousands of products for the female golfer from famous makers such as Marcia Hanasport, Elandale, Sunderland, Footjoy, Lady Fairway, Etonic, Nancy Lopez, Waterford & more.
Wood Carvers Supply®, Inc.	Everything for the woodcarver, since 1955. Over 2000 quality products including knives, hand & power tools, books, videos & much more! We are experts & lead our industry with top quality innovative products, service & value. Many of our products are developed by & available only from us; all are guaranteed for satisfaction & lowest price.
Woodburning Tools By Colwood	Professional, high-quality woodburning tools & accessories for pyrographers, as well as woodcarvers who specialize in wildlife artistry.
Woodworker's Library	Hundreds of books & videos on all types of woodworking from carving to tuning, carpentry, joinery & even carriage-making.
Worldwide Marketing – World of Products	A large variety of gifts & collectibles including figurines, sculptures, candles, jewelry, home décor brass, crystal & novelties.
Wyoming Buffalo Company	Original & distinctive Western gourmet gifts made up of buffalo meats, smoked buffalo sausages & jerky.
1stGift.com	Great gourmet food baskets available for shipping within the United States.

Catalog City is adding new catalogs & functionality all the time. This is intended to be a representation of the Catalog City Partner Store site. Please visit the Partner Store to see the current offerings.

Store	Type of Merchandise
20th Century Plastics Office & Photo Organizers	Office & photo storage & filing systems, including photo/slide pages, photo albums, vinyl envelopes & bags, diskette & CD storage systems, report covers & file folders.
247 Gifts	Gourmet food & theme baskets that can be shipped to U.S. destinations. Theme baskets make the perfect gift for anyone on your list including children, sports fans, movie buffs, new parents, health nuts, gardeners, country cookers & pasta lovers. There are also baskets for chocolate connoisseurs, tub soakers, coffee drinkers, business associates, birthdays & all kinds of special celebrations.

CLICK 12   MY QUIXTAR

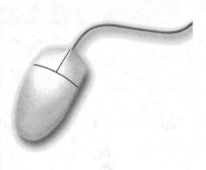

CLICK HERE TO ACCESS YOUR PRIVATE QUIXTAR PAGE. YOU DECIDE WHAT INFORMATION YOU WANT TO SEE. Q-CREDITS FOR MEMBERS. VOLUME FOR THE IBO ORGANIZATIONS YOU CHOOSE. YOU PICK THE NEWS YOU WANT. THE SPORTS YOU WANT. THE WEATHER YOU WANT. THE STOCKS YOU WANT. FIND THE MAPS YOU WANT. BECAUSE MY QUIXTAR IS ALL ABOUT GETTING MORE OF WHAT YOU WANT.

MY QUIXTAR

YOUR PERSONALIZED WEB PAGE

Do you ever wonder how top executives stay informed on all the topics that are important to their day-to-day success? What's going on with their company, from the moment they wake up in the morning, to the time they go to bed. How the stock market is doing. Who their top producers are. What their partners are up to. The late-breaking news stories. Who won the game last night while they were out closing a big business deal.

How is it that they always manage to show up prepared for the local weather, whether they're traveling across town, or across the country? And arrive at their destination without having to stop and ask directions.

These successful business people do not do it alone. They have a staff of personal assistants who brief them on all the important issues. The top news stories. The market. Even the weather.

Now you can benefit from the same kind of personalized information. Without having to hire a bevy of assistants. Because you have Quixtar. **My Quixtar**.

Just check in with **My Quixtar**, any time of day or night, to get the latest information you want. And need. To stay on top of your business. And your life.

Here you'll find **Headline News** from the **AP Business Wire, AP Domestic News**, and **AP Sports**. **Weather**, for your local area, and in any U.S. city. Customized **Maps** to get you where you need to go. Up-to-the-minute **Stock Quotes**. For just the stocks you want to follow. Current arrangements with your **Network Savings Partners**. **PV/BV Profiles** for IBOs. **Q-Credits** available for redemption for Members. It's all here for you at **My Quixtar**.

EDIT PROFILE

When Members or IBOs click on **My Quixtar** in the navy blue navigational bar at the top of your screen, you'll be greeted by a customizable page with seven sections. When you set up your profile, you can choose which sections you want to see, how much information you'll get in each section, and even where each section shows up on your screen. Some sections give you more custom options that let you specify exactly what information you want reported to you. No more wading through pages of stock prices to find the prices on the stocks you follow. Get only what you want, how you want it, and where you want it with **My Quixtar**.

When you click on Edit Profile, you will see **My Quixtar Profile Setup**. Listed on the left side of your screen will be the seven components of **My Quixtar: Headline News, Maps, Network Savings Partners, PV/BV, Quixtar News, Stock**, and **Weather**. Members will see **Member Rewards** instead of **PV/BV**. Clients cannot access **My Quixtar**. It is a service provided exclusively for Members and IBOs.

 **Members Only**   Clients who want to access **My Quixtar** can become Members. Click on **Member Perks** to **Learn More**. Members who want to earn PV/BV, instead of Q-Credits, can register as an IBO & still access **My Quixtar**. Click on **Income Options** to **Register as an IBO**.

Let's look at each one of these seven sections to see how you can customize them to your liking.

HEADLINE NEWS

Click on Headline News. You'll find three types of news available to you: **AP Business News**, **AP Domestic News**, and **AP Sports**. Once you decide which ones you want to see on your **My Quixtar** page, place a checkmark in the box next to that item by pointing to the box with your mouse and clicking. This will make that section **Visible** on your page. Next, decide how many headlines you would like to see at any one time in each section. Click on the arrow in the drop-down box and select the number to display.

You may also choose to change the order in which the news sections appear. If you want to do this, click Reorder. Highlight the section you want to move, by clicking on it. Once it's highlighted, click on the up or down arrows to reposition it on your screen. When you get it just the way you like it, click Back to save your changes and return to the previous screen. Now, click Finish to return to **My Quixtar**. The changes you've made will be reflected immediately.

To read a news story, just click on its headline. You'll see the time and date of the story, and be able to read it right on your screen. When you're finished, click on Back to My Quixtar.

You can also see stories from the past week by clicking on the History button. This is a nice feature to use if you've been traveling and don't want to plow through a pile of newspapers when you return.

QUIXTAR NEWS

You'll also keep up-to-date on what's new in the word of Quixtar by using this section to customize your **Quixtar News**. This works just like the **Headline News** section. Click on Edit Profile, then Quixtar News. Check off the Sections you want to be **Visible**, specify the Number to Display, **Reorder** if you want, and then click Finish. You'll find a **History** button here, too.

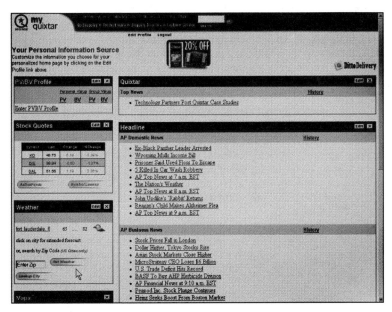

FIGURE 12-1   MY QUIXTAR

MAPS

If you want to access custom maps from your **My Quixtar** page, place a checkmark in the box next to Maps. Now, go ahead and click on Finish & Return to My Quixtar and take a look at how the maps work. In the **Maps** section, type in your **Address**, including street address, **City**, **State**, **Province** (for Canadians only) and **Zip Code** (for USA only).

Now, click on Get Map. This will link you to the MapQuest site, where you can get driving directions. First, you'll see a street map of the area surrounding the address you specified. The exact location you typed in will be marked with a gold star.

Now, click on Directions From if you want to know how to get from your address to a friend's house. You'll see your address, already filled out in the **Enter Starting Address** section. Go ahead and type your friend's address in the section called **Enter Destination Address**. Then, click on Get Directions. You'll get **Direction Results** that tell you the **Total Distance** to their house and **the Total Estimated Time** to drive there. You'll also see a road map from point-to-point, with the recommended route highlighted for you. Below the map, you'll find turn-by-turn **Directions** from your house to theirs.

You'll have several **Directions Options** on the left side of your screen. You can click Printer-Friendly Page to print out the map and directions to take with you in the car. Or, if you prefer the paperless version, click Download to PDA to transfer the information to a handheld device, like a Palm™. Or, click on Fax Directions to send them to a friend. You'll also want to get directions for the way back home. To do that, simply click on Reverse Directions.

When you are done using the maps, close the MapQuest window by clicking on the X in the top right corner of your screen. Now you are back at the **My Quixtar** page.

STOCK QUOTES

Another way to edit your profile is to click on the Edit button in the section you want to change. Try it now. In the **Stock Quotes** section, click on Edit. This will take you to the **Stock Editor**. If you know the ticker symbol you want to track, click in the Current Stock Symbols box and type it in. Be sure to use a space to separate each symbol from other symbols you may already have in the box. If you know the name of the company, but don't know the ticker symbol, click on Lookup Symbol. Enter the company's name in the box provided and click Go. You'll see a list of companies, and their ticker symbols, that match your request. Click on the one you want, and you'll be able to review all kinds of statistics on that stock. You'll find out its opening price today, the high and low price, the 52 week high and low, earnings per share, the number of shares outstanding, the P/E ratio, its market capitalization, the exchange it's traded on and more.

Now, click on My Quixtar to return to your personal page. If you want to delete a stock from your portfolio report, go back into Edit. Highlight the stock's ticker symbol, and click once on your right mouse button. Choose Delete. The stock will disappear from your list. When you have your stocks set up just the way you want them, click Save or Finish & Return to My Quixtar. Either way, you'll be back at your personal page.

WEATHER

You'll really appreciate this section, where you can track the weather in up to five U.S. cities at a time. Click on Edit and then enter the **zip codes** of the areas you want to track. If you don't know the zip code, click on Lookup City. Now, type in the name of the **City** and the abbreviation for its **State** and click Lookup Zip Code. The correct zip code will appear in the box labeled **Looked up zip code**. Now, you can enter that zip code into one of the five Current Zip Codes boxes. When you're done, click Finish to return to your **Profile Setup** and then Finish & Return to My Quixtar.

The cities you requested are now listed in the **Weather** section, along with their forecasts for today. To see an extended forecast, click on the city. You'll find a three-day forecast, along with options for viewing temperatures in **Celsius**, and seeing **Radar** or **Satellite** images. Click on Finish & Return to My Quixtar.

You're not limited to weather forecasts in just those five cities. If you want to know the weather in another city, just highlight the words Enter Zip in the box provided. Now, click Get Weather. And there, you will have it! Or, click on Lookup City, just below the **Enter Zip** box, and you can get the weather that way.

NETWORK SAVINGS PARTNERS

This is a nifty little section that gives you convenient links to your **Network Savings Partners**. Here, you'll find travel partners, office equipment and services partners, automotive services partners, insurance partners and more. Click on any one of these partners to get specifics on your special pricing plans, toll-free reservations numbers, and links to their private Web sites.

 **It's Payback Time**   Members & IBOs will find that they can quickly recoup their Quixtar registration fee just by taking advantage of the special pricing offered by these **Network Savings Partners**. Carry your Quixtar ID card in your wallet, so you'll never miss out on an opportunity for these savings.

You can choose to remove this section from your **My Quixtar** page simply by clicking on the X at the top of the **Network Savings Partners** box. But, we wouldn't recommend it. Why hide such a good thing?

PV/BV PROFILE

Yes, we've saved the best for last. If you're an IBO, this section will show you your volume for the current business month. You'll always know where you stand, and what your leaders are up to. One click, on either Edit or Enter PVBV Profile, will take you to the **PV/BV Editor**. Here, you'll enter the **IBO Numbers** of up to ten organizations you want to track volume on. There's a space for you to type in their **Names**, too. When you're done, click on Save.

Anytime you want an update on your volume, just click on the gray Update button. You'll get current **Personal** and **Group Volume** for each organization you've specified. Plus your own overall volume as well. And you'll see a reminder note to let you know the last date and time you retrieved your volume updates.

So you'll always be up-to-date on what's going on in your business. Isn't that brilliant?

MEMBER REWARDS

If you're a Member, you'll have a special section called **Member Rewards**. Here, you'll find your **Q-Credits Accumulated**. Click on the gray Update box to get your most current totals. There's also a handy link for you to Go to the Redemption Center. That's where you'll see all the goodies you can get by trading in your Q-Credits.

You'll find lots of cool items in Q-Credit categories ranging from 1001-3000, all the way up to 60,000. Or, exchange your Q-Credits for Frequent Flyer Miles on most major airlines with the **ClickRewards™** program. The choice is up to you. After all, that's what **My Quixtar** is all about. More choices. Just for you.

CLICK 13   MEMBER PERKS

CLICK HERE TO JOIN AN EXCLUSIVE ONLINE COMMUNITY WHERE YOU'LL SAVE MONEY. AND EARN REWARDS. ENJOY THE BENEFITS OF MEMBERSHIP. USE A QUIXTAR VISA AND MULTIPLY YOUR REWARDS EVEN FASTER. THEN REDEEM THEM FOR CLICKMILES™ TRAVEL AWARDS. OR FOR PREMIUM MERCHANDISE. BECAUSE MEMBERSHIP HAS ITS PERKS.

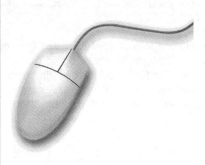

MEMBER PERKS

INTRO TO PERKS

Everyone likes to save money. And time. But when you can get goodies in the process, it's even better. That's what you'll experience if you register as a Quixtar Member. At the moment, you can register for just $19.95. That covers your membership for the first year. Renewing after that costs even less. Now, let's take a look at what that gets you.

Click on Member Perks in the navy blue navigational bar, and then click on Learn More. You'll see the **Intro to Perks**. This tells you what you'll get for your $19.95. **Member Pricing**, on every product Quixtar sells. **Member Rewards** in the form of Q-Credits. Get 2000 Q-Credits for signing on as a U.S. member, or 3000 Q-Credits for signing on as a Canadian member. Continue to earn Q-Credits with each **Partner Store** purchase. Redeem those Q-Credits for special premium merchandise. Or, trade them in for ClickMiles™. ClickMiles™ can be used for travel benefits on most major U.S. airlines.

You'll have access to **My Quixtar** where you can create your own custom Web page. You'll also enjoy **Network Savings** on a variety of business services. Plus, take advantage of **Awesome Offers** for members only.

FIGURE 13-1 MEMBER PERKS

MEMBER PRICING

If you like saving money, then you'll love being a Quixtar Member. Take a look at the type of savings you can expect. Click on Continue at the bottom of the page, or Member Pricing at the top, to see Member savings of up to 30% on things you use everyday. These are not cheap generic brands. These are top-quality products backed by the **Quixtar Exclusives** one-year satisfaction guarantee.

MEMBER REWARDS

Next, click on Continue, or Member Rewards, for a glimpse of the **Partner Stores** where Members will **Earn Q-Credits**. For a list of **Partner Stores**, see *Click 10, Partner Stores*, in this guidebook. Members earn Q-Credits on every purchase from the **Partner Stores**. And, you'll be assured of getting the best price that these companies offer on the Web.

On your screen, you'll also see a sampling of items that you can get when you **Redeem Q-Credits**.

 **Double Your Treasure**   U.S. Members will earn Q-Credits even faster when you use the Quixtar Visa® Rewards Card. With it, you'll earn 2 Q-Credits for every $1 spent on your Quixtar purchases and 1 extra Q-Credit on each $1 spent on all other purchases, no matter where you shop. Plus, these Members earn an extra 1000 Q-Credits when they apply for the card online. Click on **Quixtar VISA® Rewards Card**, on the front page of **Member Perks**, to find out more.

MY QUIXTAR

Go ahead and click on Continue, or My Quixtar, to see how you can set up your own custom home page, for keeping tabs on your world. With **My Quixtar**, you'll be able to stay in touch with your choice of news, sports, weather, stocks, and more. See *Click 12, My Quixtar*, in this guidebook for complete details on creating your personal page.

You'll be able to keep track of the latest Quixtar specials, promotions, and news articles here, too.

NETWORK SAVINGS

Now, click on Continue, or Network Savings to find more ways your Quixtar membership will save you money. You'll probably earn back your membership fee, just by taking advantage of one of the great savings opportunities offered by the **Network Savings Partners**. These partners offer you great pricing on a wide array of services for your business and personal travel, insurance, automotive, and business equipment needs.

ARE YOU READY

This time, when you click on Continue, you'll have the chance to **Become a Quixtar Member** and get your free Q-Credits. If you're ready, click on Yes! to **Register Now**.

REGISTER NOW

The next step is to enter the **Quixtar number** of the person who referred you to this site. There is a box at the top of the page where you can click and type in this number. Click on the gray Continue box to move on.

The personal touch is an important part of the Quixtar experience, so **If you were not referred to Quixtar**, click on click here to request an IBO referral number. When you do, you'll see an **IBO Referral Number Request** screen. Type in your **Name** and **Zip** in the boxes provided. Click in the appropriate circle to indicate whether you'd like to be contacted via Telephone or Email. Now, click the gray Send box to go on. You'll see a message that tells you you'll receive a referring IBO number within 1-2 business days. We requested to be contacted by email and found that we received a referring IBO number within minutes.

You'll see a membership application form, which you can complete by clicking in each box and typing in the required **information**. You'll be asked to create a **password** here, which will ensure that only you can access your Member account. When you are finished, click on the gray Continue button.

You'll be provided with a list of **Member Terms and Conditions** on the following page. You may want to print this out for future reference. Then, click on Continue.

The next screen will ask for your **Payment Information**. Click in the boxes provided and type in your **information**. Remember, this information will be encrypted for security before it is sent to Quixtar. Click on Continue.

Congratulations, you've just created a member account with Quixtar. Now you'll see your **Member number** and **password**. Print this out, as you'll be referring to it frequently.

Now, there's just one more detail to take care of. Place your mouse pointer on Click here to download. When you click this, you'll open up a **Membership Registration Form** that you'll need to sign, complete, and mail in to Quixtar, to be sure your membership is processed correctly. You'll be able to enjoy the benefits of membership immediately, but don't forget to mail in that form.

PRIVACY POLICY

Giving out your personal information, whether to a catalog company, or an online merchant, can mean a lot of unwanted junk mail is headed your way. But not with Quixtar. Click on Privacy Policy, just below the navy blue navigational bar to read about how Quixtar will never share your information with Third Parties, Quixtar's use of **Cookies**, and more. You'll rest easier knowing what we know.

REDEMPTION CENTER

Let's go back to the **Member Perks** front page and take a look at the goodies that await you in the **Redemption Center**. Just like with frequent flyer miles, Q-Credits can be redeemed at a wide range of point levels. You'll be surprised at how nice the merchandise is, even at the lowest level of Q-Credits.

Recently, we saw a Crystal Ensemble for only 2900 Q-Credits. It included a crystal lamp, vase, and pair of candlesticks. Remember, you'll earn that amount, and more, just for registering as a Member and applying for the Quixtar VISA® Rewards Card. The next level offered a Fishing Rod & Reel Combo for 5400 Q-Credits. One level up from that, we found an 11-piece Stainless Steel Cookware Set for 10,400 Q-Credits. A beautiful new Panasonic Microwave Oven caught our eye in the next level at 20,400 Q-Credits. At 30,400 Q-Credits, we found the Diamond

Necklace hard to resist. In the top level, we found a Wide-Screen Television for 50,400 Q-Credits.

These items represent just some of the many choices available to Members in each of the levels of the **Redemption Center**. Check back here frequently to see the newest additions to the goodies you'll have to choose from when you redeem your Q-Credits.

To check your **Q-Credits Balance**, look at the top left of your **Redemption Center** screen. Here you'll see the number of Q-Credits you've earned. To be sure your balance includes any recent purchases you've made, click on Refresh Q-Credits.

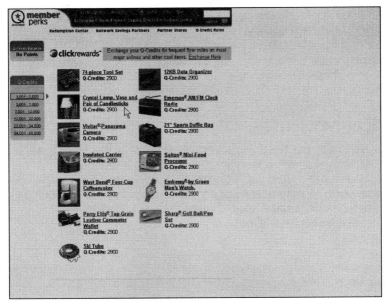

FIGURE 13-2   REDEMPTION CENTER

To order your free Q-Credit merchandise, locate the item you want and click on Add to cart. You'll proceed through the checkout, passing through the screens for **Shopping Cart**, **Shipping**

Information, and **Order Preview**, and **Finalize Order**. As you
see each screen appear, just click on the red Continue to Checkout
box, until you arrive at the **Order Preview** screen. This time,
click on the red Finalize Purchase box. Look! There's no cost
information on these screens because you're using your Q-Credits.
The number of Q-Credits used will appear on these screens as
Points.

And remember, Members can exchange their Q-Credits for
ClickMiles™, which are good for free travel on most major U.S.
airlines, if they prefer. To exchange your Q-Credits for
ClickMiles™, click on Exchange Here, at the top of the
Redemption Center screen. From the next page, you can also
click on FAQs to view the **FAQ for Quixtar Member Perks'
ClickRewards™ Program**.

The **FAQs** page has a link to the **ClickRewards**™ site, where you
can get a status report on the number of **ClickMiles**™ you've
earned.

Q CREDIT RULES

While you're in the **Redemption Center**, click on Q-Credit Rules,
located at the top of your screen, just below the navy blue
navigational bar. Here you'll find all the nitty-gritty on how Q-
Credits work.   Remember, you decide whether to redeem your Q-
Credits for merchandise, or exchange them for **ClickMiles**™.
Either way, you'll be smiling!

CLICK 14   INCOME OPTIONS

CLICK HERE TO LAUNCH YOUR OWN INTERNET-BASED BUSINESS. POWERED BY QUIXTAR. TEAM UP WITH THE BEST OF THE BEST. CATCH THE TECHNOLOGY WAVE. PROFIT FROM THE EXPLOSIVE GROWTH OF ONLINE SHOPPING. BE IN BUSINESS FOR YOURSELF. BUT NEVER BY YOURSELF. THE WORLD IS WAITING. FOR YOU. AND FOR QUIXTAR.

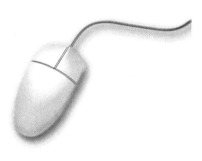

INCOME OPTIONS

EXTRA INCOME

Just saying those words can help you feel better. Breathe easier. Take some pressure off. Open up your choices. Free up some time. After all, who wouldn't like some **Extra Income**, no matter what their financial situation?

But until now, extra income usually meant taking a second job. Or a third. And that can take its toll on you. Of course, you could always start your own business. If you only had the money. And the experience. But the risks are high. Most small businesses fail. Only a few of them last through the first five years.

Now you have another option. An **Income Option** all its own. The time is right for making money on the Internet. The time is right for Quixtar. This may just be your vehicle to the life you've always dreamed of having.

Click on Income Options in the navy blue navigational bar, then click on Hows & Whys of Extra Income to view a short slide presentation of the benefits of becoming an Independent Business Owner affiliated with Quixtar. Look for the Forward button on the bottom of each slide, and click on it to go on to the next page. When you're done, click on Register as an Independent Business Owner. Or, if you want to skip the slide show, just click on IBO Registration at the top of the page.

Figure 14-1

IBO Registration

On the first screen you'll see, answer the question about which country you'll be operating your business in, by clicking on either **United States** or **Canada**. Next, you'll see a screen where you need to provide some information. Click in the Referring IBO # box, and type in the **number** of the person who referred you to the site. You'll also need to click in the Key box, and type in the first three letters of their last name. Then, click on Continue.

Hey, Vicki, Don't Lose That Number In order to become an IBO, you need to have someone affiliated with Quixtar refer you. The strength of this business is that you always have people vitally interested in helping you succeed. If you don't know anyone affiliated with Quixtar, please call 1-800-222-1462 for the name of someone near you.

Next, select your Birthdate from the drop-down boxes, and type your **E-mail address** in the box provided. Click on Continue.

Then, complete the **Individual Registrant Information** on the next screen by clicking in each box provided and typing in the requested **information** for you, and your spouse, if applicable. Also, complete the **Contact Information** in the same way. Finally, set-up your **Account Information** by choosing a **Password**. Retype your **Password** in the box labeled **Verify Password**. Go ahead and fill out the **Password Hint Question** and **Password Hint Answer**. These will be used later, to help you remember your **Password**, in case you forget it. Click on Continue.

If you've had an IBO # previously, click on Yes, on the next screen. Type in **the previous IBO#**, and select Your last date of activity from the drop-down box provided. If this doesn't apply to you, just click on Continue to go on.

That's it for the **Information Gathering**. Click Continue on the next screen, to read the **Independent Business Ownership Plan**. When you are done, click Continue.

Indicate your desire to apply for IBO status by clicking Yes, I would like to apply, on the next screen. Then, click on Continue.

Read about **the important whereas and wherefores** on the next screen in the **Quixtar Terms and Conditions**. Click Continue to agree to them and move on.

You're almost official! As of today, you'll be registered as an IBO for a cost of $99.95, plus tax and shipping. That includes your choice of a special start-up selection of product. There are three packages for you to pick from: the **Intro Pack**, the **Health Pack**, and the **Self Pack**. Select click here for detail if you'd like to review the contents of each pack. Place a checkmark in the box nearest your choice by clicking the box with your mouse.

If you'd like your selection to be sent to an address other than the one shown, go ahead and type in the proper **Shipping Info** by double-clicking and typing in the boxes provided. Click on Continue.

Your Total Order will show on the next screen. Enter **Your Payment Information** by clicking in the circle to indicate your Credit Card Type. Then, click and type your **Name** and **Credit Card Number** in the boxes provided. Select your Expiration Date from the drop-down boxes. And click Continue.

Way to go! You're an IBO! The next screen will show you your **Quixtar IBO number** and **Your Password**. You'll also see **The Invoice # for Your Start-up Pack**. This would be a good page to print out.   And while you're printing, be sure to click on the links for BSMAA and Contract Link at the bottom of your screen. It's important that your **Registration Agreement** be completed, signed and mailed within 30 days to ensure you remain an active IBO. So go ahead and print these out now and get them sent in while it's fresh in your mind. Read and sign them, then follow the directions for mailing. Click on Continue.

Now that you're all official, go over and check your email. You'll find your first official piece of business correspondence in your mailbox. What do you think it could be? It's an email confirmation for your Start-up Pack.

Welcome to this incredible online business!

PRIVACY POLICY

You'll be glad to know that there is a very specific Privacy Policy that lets you know how your personal information will be used by Quixtar. It's called **The Quixtar Pledge**. You can read it by clicking on Privacy Policy at the top of your screen, just below the navy blue navigational bar. You'll rest easier knowing that your information will not be sold to Third Parties. That means your mailbox won't be filling up with lots of stuff you don't want. Because Quixtar gives you more of what you want. Not what you don't.

CLICK 15   VIRTUAL OFFICE

CLICK HERE TO CHECK IN WITH YOUR OFFICE. YOUR VIRTUAL OFFICE. NO COMMUTE. NO BOSS. NO TIME CLOCK. ALL THE INFORMATION IBOS NEED TO RUN THIS BUSINESS IS RIGHT AT YOUR FINGERTIPS. DO BUSINESS WHENEVER YOU WANT. WHEREVER YOU WANT. WITH WHOMEVER YOU WANT. NOW THAT'S A BUSINESS!

VIRTUAL OFFICE

VIRTUAL OFFICE TOUR

Remember your first day at a new job? You probably arrived early, all excited about starting with your new company. But you may remember feeling a bit uncomfortable, too. Everyone else, it seemed, knew their way around. Everyone but you. Chances are, someone was assigned to take you around the office, on a little tour. You met lots of new people. Walked down lots of hallways. Tried to get a feel for the place. But it was all so unfamiliar to you. You wondered if you'd ever feel at home there. And eventually, you did. But it took some time.

Give yourself some time to get comfortable with your new Virtual Office. Chances are, you've never had a **Virtual Office** before. It's quite a bit different, isn't it? No building to commute to. No rush hour traffic to fight. Why, you can even do business in your bathrobe, if you want. It's all up to you.

But this office does have everything you'll need to run your business. You'll see. You probably have lots of questions already. Good. Because you'll find lots of answers here. Click on Virtual Office in the navy blue navigational bar. Now, click on Frequently Asked Questions. See, we bet a lot of the answers you were looking for are right here. Let's go back up front for a few minutes. Click on your Back button.

Take a look around. Over there, on the left. See the **Quick Links**. They've put the things you do a lot, right up front. You'll find **Quick Order, Ditto Delivery, LOS, PV/BV Inquiry, PV/BV Transfer, Business Forms** and **Tax Forms** close at hand to make it easy for you to find them. We'll cover each of these items in detail in a few minutes. For now, just remember you've got shortcuts to these items right here.

You'll find other important information up front, too. Like a list of What's New at Quixtar. Click on one of these links and you'll get a full briefing on that topic. These items include new product releases, services, and new business support materials. **Achievers** are listed here, too. Now, let's finish looking around your office.

WHAT'S NEW

You want your office to provide you with the most current, late-breaking information, without getting bogged down with all the details. You're going to like this next section. It's called **What's New**. This is a short little bulletin that keeps you up-to-date on the latest happenings in the areas of **FYI, Achievers, Business, Products, Services, Catalog, Promotions, Support Materials, Legal & Regulatory,** and **How to Connect**.

You can glance at this info in just a few minutes and come away knowing all the latest news. To get to it, begin at the navy blue navigational bar, click on Virtual Office, and then What's New. Each news bite will have a link you can click to get more detailed information on any topic you wish to review further.

FIGURE 15-1   VIRTUAL OFFICE

SERVICES

Check out the **Services** section to take advantage of great deals on **Amvox** Global Communications, **Gateway**® computer systems, **STAR** (Strategic Tax Audit Representation), the **Auto Network**, and the **New IBO VISA Card**. Each one of these services can add value to your independent business. To get there, begin at the navy blue navigational bar, click on Virtual Office, and then Services.

EDIT PROFILE

Last, but not least, there is a section in **Virtual Office** that allows you to change your personal profile information. Begin at the navy blue navigational bar, click on Virtual Office, then Edit Profile.

You'll be able to change your personal information in the areas of **Shopping**, **My Quixtar**, **General**, and **Virtual Office**.

Take a look at the **Edit Profile** choices at the top of your screen. The **Shopping** profile takes you to a screen where you can find links to update your Ditto Delivery profile and your answers to My Assessment in My Home, My Health and My Self.   The **My Quixtar** profile takes you to a screen where you can change your preferences on your customized **My Quixtar** page. The **General** profile takes you to a Customer Service screen where you can change your password, your street address, your email address, telephone numbers and more. **Virtual Office** profiles can be changed in the **My Business** section of the site. Or click on Help to receive further assistance in any of these **Edit Profile** categories.

LOGOUT

When you've put in your time at the **Virtual Office**, you can logout before you leave. This will keep your business information private, so it won't be accessible by anyone else who walks by your computer. Think of it as the equivalent of locking the door before you leave to go home. But you probably are already home. So all you need to do is logout. Go up to the navy blue navigational bar and click on Logout.

That completes the first part of the tour of your **Virtual Office**. The next two chapters will introduce you to the rest of the Virtual Office features found in **Product Ordering** and **My Business**. Isn't is good to know that your office is staffed and open for business 24 hours a day, 7 days a week, whether you're at home, lying on the beach, or spending time with the people that matter most in your life. What a place you've got there!

CLICK 16 PRODUCT ORDERING

CLICK HERE TO EXPLORE SPECIAL PRODUCT-RELATED FEATURES THAT ARE RESERVED JUST FOR IBOs. ENTER LARGE PRODUCT ORDERS WITH THE MULTI-LINE FORM. MANAGE YOUR DITTO DELIVERY PORTFOLIO. TAP INTO MARKETING TIPS. AND MEETING SUPPORT. ALL DESIGNED TO HELP YOU GROW A STRONG AND PROFITABLE BUSINESS.

PRODUCT ORDERING

PRODUCT ORDERING

As an IBO, you're a busy person. And you've got a business to run. You know what you want. Stock numbers. Case lots. Literature and business support materials. You want a **Quick Order** experience. You've come to the right place.

You want to streamline your business. Eliminate repetitive tasks. Free up more time. So you can be out with your people. Building your business. **Ditto Delivery** is for you. It lets you schedule a standing order of the products you use most frequently.

To help you increase your volume, you'll find **Marketing Tips**. New ideas. Tried and true strategies. Tips on connecting with your target customers. Handling objections. And asking for the order.

Platinum business leaders have more responsibility. For training.
Promoting. Introducing new products. You'll find what you need
in **Meeting Support**.

So relax. Everything you need to help you move product more
easily is right here in this area of your **Virtual Office**. Let's take a
look at how it works.

QUICK ORDER

When you need to order a lot of items and you want to do it
quickly, you'll turn to the Multi-Line Order feature time and time
again. To get there, begin at the Home Page and click on View
Cart. Look over on the right side of your screen and click on Multi-
Line Form. Now, click in the first Qty box and enter your desired
quantity. Next, click in the first SKU box and type in the **stock
number** you want to order. Keep on entering your order
information this way for each item on your list. When you're done,
click on Add to Cart. Then, Check Out as usual. That's quick and
easy, isn't it?

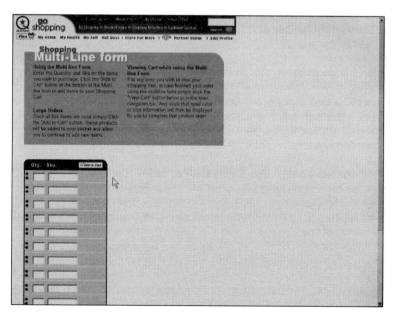

FIGURE 16-1   MULTI-LINE FORM

Keep Tabs on Things   Experienced computer users like to take shortcuts whenever possible. Here's one you'll use a lot. Let's say you're filling out a form on your screen. It's got boxes for you to type in all the pertinent information. Whenever you want to move from one box to another, just press the **Tab** button to move your mouse cursor to the next box. And, if you want to go backwards through the boxes, press and hold down the **Shift** key while you press and release the **Tab** key. Now you're in the know. What a pro!

DITTO DELIVERY℠ – THE BASICS

If you're like us, you'd jump at an alternative to running out to the store to get the things that you're running out of at home. You know, stuff that you use up all the time and have to replace. Stuff like coffee, shampoo, vitamins, and bathroom tissue. Dog food, kitty litter, light bulbs, and trash bags. Cosmetics, aspirin, cereal, and pasta.

Wouldn't it be great if you could have all that stuff show up at your door, just when you need it? Well, now you can. With **Ditto Delivery**, a complimentary service of Quixtar. **Ditto Delivery** lets you schedule a standing order for the stuff you use the most, like personal care items, food and nutritional supplements, and household cleaners.

You set the schedule. Use **Ditto Delivery** for just a couple of things, or for everything you possibly can. Personally, the more we use **Ditto Delivery**, the more we like it. Just think of what you could do with all that time you'll save, not running back and forth to the store.

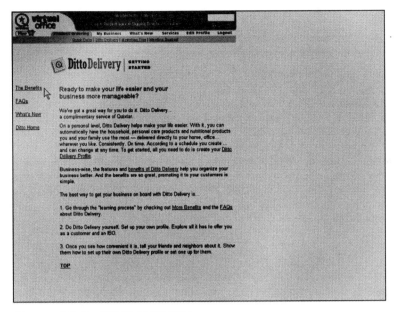

FIGURE 16-2   DITTO DELIVERY

Okay, you're ready to give it a whirl. Here's what you do. In the navy blue navigational bar, click on Virtual Office, then Product Ordering, then Ditto Delivery. Now, look on the left side of your screen and you'll see Getting Started. Click on that first. Look over this page and follow its links to check out **The Benefits**, **FAQs**, and **What's New**.

Now, you're ready to do your own **Ditto Delivery** profile. Click on Ditto Home, or use your Back button to get back to the **Welcome to Ditto Delivery** page. Look on the right side of your screen and you'll see Create a new Ditto Delivery profile. Click on it. Now, you'll be looking at a **Customer Profile** form. Go ahead and complete the information needed to set up your profile. In the **IBO Information** section, click in the Ordering IBO# box and type in your own **IBO#**. The Volume IBO# box is used to give another IBO credit for the volume associated with this order profile. If you are doing this profile for an IBO in your

organization, enter **their IBO#** here, otherwise enter your own
IBO#. Remember to use your Tab key to move forward from box
to box.

In the **Profile Information** section, select Active from the drop-
down menu by clicking on the down arrow and highlighting it with
your mouse. Next, you'll get to choose the Process day of the
month. This is the calendar date, each month, when your **Ditto
Delivery** order will be processed. Choose whichever date works
best for you. Most people prefer to choose a date early in the
month, so they don't find themselves with more month than
money. Your actual order will ship on the next scheduled ship day
following that date. In the next box, select a Shipping method.
Standard shipping usually works fine, since you're planning for
your delivery to arrive before you run out of products.

Next, complete the **Client or Ship-To Information**. In the first
box, enter the **Ship-to IMC#**. This is the identification number
that was given to an IBO, Member, or Client, when they first
registered with Quixtar. In the next box, type in the **Ship-to
Name**. If this is your personal profile, fill in your own name here.
Now, complete the **Address Line 1** and **Address Line 2** boxes,
along with the **City**, **State** and **Zip**. There are also boxes for your
Phone Number and **E-mail**.

To finish up your profile, provide your **Billing Information**. Enter
your credit **Card Number** without dashes and without spaces.
Select the month and year of your Expiration Date by clicking the
down arrows in the drop-down boxes. Click in the last box and
type in the **Cardholder's Name**. Read the confirmation note at
the bottom of your screen and click Add Profile to continue.

You'll be given a **Profile #** for future reference. You don't really
need to write it down because **Virtual Office** will keep a record of
it for you. Whenever you want to make changes to your profile,
you can do it from any one of three areas of the site. You can
access it through the **Go Shopping** section, the **Edit Profile**
section, or the **Virtual Office**.

I Want One, Too Members and Clients can create, monitor and change their own profiles just like you can. They'll edit their profiles through Go Shopping. You may want to create a profile with them. It's a nice service to offer as part of your business. High-touch. With high-tech. What a winning combination!

Now that you've got a **Ditto Delivery** profile, you'll want to know how to **Manage a specific Ditto Profile**. Go back to the **Ditto Home**, either by clicking on Home , just below the navy blue navigational bar, or by using your Back button. Look on the right side of your screen and you'll see a box labeled **Enter Profile Number.** So, go ahead and enter your profile number . Select View/Update profile information from the drop-down box and click Go!

The next screen you'll see is the **Profile Detail**. Here you'll find all of the information you provided earlier. If you've set up a **Product Schedule**, you'll see that here, too. Click on Change Shipping/Billing Info if you want to make any changes to this information. This will show you the **Profile Info Update** screen. Find the box that contains the information you want to change and click inside the box. This will highlight the information you have there. Type in your **new information** and the old information will go away. When you are done making changes, click on the Submit Changes button at the bottom of the page.

Now, look up at the top of your screen, just below the navy blue navigational bar. You'll notice that a new row of menu choices has appeared below **Ditto Delivery**. You can click on any of these links to navigate your way through the other features of **Ditto Delivery**.

In a few minutes, we'll take a closer look at some of these great features. But first, let's schedule some deliveries for you. Go back to the **Profile Detail** and click on Change Product Schedule . The next screen you'll see is called **Product Scheduler**. Click in the box labeled Enter new SKU and type in a **stock number** you'd like to schedule for **Ditto Delivery**. Remember to use a **W** prefix if you want an each, rather than a case. If applicable, click in the size/color box and type in the **codes** for what you want. Click on Add Item and you'll see that item show up on the **Current Product Schedule** at the bottom of your screen.

Next, click on the EDIT link that you see to the left of the stock number. Now, you'll see the **Product Maintenance** page. This shows you the **SKU**, **Description**, and **PV/BV**. There's a section here for Price, too. Click in one of the three price circles to select the price that will be charged for this product. The **IBO/Member** price and the **List price** appear automatically. If you'd rather charge a different price, select Other and type in the **price** you want to charge.

Now, select the Start Date from the drop-down menu boxes. Fill in the monthly schedule by typing in the **quantity** you want to have sent to you each month. If you don't want any sent in certain months, type a **0** in those boxes. Then click on Update Item. If you want to remove an item, select yes from the drop-down menu box that asks Do you want to remove this item? Click on the Remove Item button and, poof, it's gone.

Are You Sure This is the Shortest Way?
About this time, you're probably wondering if this **Ditto Delivery** is really a time-saver after all. It seems to take a lot of steps to get this all set-up. We agree with you. It does take some time to set it up the way you want it. But once you do, the time savings and convenience you'll enjoy by having stuff delivered when you need it will make it all worthwhile. If you want, take a juice break and come back in a little while when you're ready to finish up.

Okay, you're back. Click on your Back button to return to the **Product Scheduler** and continue adding **SKU** numbers and setting up monthly delivery schedules for each item you want.

Keep in mind, the time you spend at your keyboard doing this is much easier than walking up and down the aisles of your local store, pulling heavy stuff off the shelves, loading it into your cart and lugging it home.

If you need some inspiration, click on Take a Look at Our Most Popular Picks for Ditto Delivery. You'll find this icon on the **Product Scheduler** page. On the **Popular Picks** pages, you'll find dozens of items you probably use in your home. There's a picture of each item, along with pricing and volume information. If you'd like to add any of these to your **Ditto Delivery** schedule, click on the Add To Ditto link next to the picture.

If you want to see the full Wholesale Price List, click on the link for View Product Price List. You'll need to have Adobe® Acrobat® Reader to use this feature. If this software's not already on your computer, click on the gold Get Acrobat Reader icon to download it free of charge.

DITTO DELIVERY℠ – THE BEST PART

Now that you've successfully set-up your own **Ditto Delivery** schedule, you're ready to enjoy the benefits that come along with it. Not only have you simplified your life, and saved oodles of time and aggravation. You've also added consistent volume to your business. Ooh, ahhh! Now you get it, right? Imagine how wonderful it would be if you shared the benefits of **Ditto Delivery** with the IBOs, Members and Clients in your organization. They'd save time. Reduce stress. And you'd all enjoy the benefits of consistent volume, month in and month out.

Let's go back to the Product Scheduler. Look at the monthly abbreviations along the top of your schedule. Each month is represented by the first letter in its name. You'll notice that all of those letters appear in color. That tells you that they're links. Pick one and click on it. The next page you'll see is the **Monthly Projection** page. It shows you the total PV/BV you'll receive for those scheduled items.

If you want to see your Annual Projection, click on that menu selection below the navy blue navigational bar. Here you'll see the

PV/BV you can expect each month, as well as the estimated cost and estimated margin. Margin means profit. To you. Ooh, ahhh!

But wait, it gets better. Go back to Ditto Home and select View group portfolio statistics in the drop-down box for Manage my profile portfolio . This brings up a page called **Group Portfolio Overview**. Take a look at the **Volume Projections**. Wow! Platinum IBOs will see the **Total projected annual sales** and **Total projected annual PV/BV** for all of your organization's Ditto Deliveries put together. How'd you like to see 7500PV in each month of the year, just from **Ditto Delivery**? See, we told you you'd love **Ditto Delivery**. Ooh, ahhh!

DITTO DELIVERY^{SM} – THE DETAILS

There's lots of other good information in **Ditto Delivery**. If you're a numbers person, you'll thrive on this stuff. If you're not, you can skip this section. All you need to know is that **Ditto Delivery** is a good thing. A very good thing. And the more people you help set-up profiles in **Ditto Delivery**, the more you'll be smiling.

Let's take a look at some of the other information available to you. Go back to the Ditto Home . See the section on the right called **Manage a Specific Ditto profile**. IBOs will be able to access profiles they've entered for themselves and their members and clients. Platinum IBOs will be able to see profiles for everyone in their organization. Go ahead and Enter a **Profile Number** and select View Maintenance History from the drop-down menu box . You'll see the **Maintenance History Overview**. This shows you every time a change was made to this profile. For more details, click on the date the change was made and you'll see all the specifics.

Or, you can select View order history from the Manage a specific Ditto profile drop-down box . You'll get the **Order History Overview** screen. This will show you every invoice that was shipped out for the profile number you specified. Click on the Invoice number link to get an even greater amount of detail on the order.

You want more reports? You've got them! Go back to Ditto Home and select View personal portfolio statistics from the **Manage my**

profile portfolio drop-down menu box. You'll find **Volume Projections** galore on this **Personal Portfolio Overview**. Or, select View group portfolio statistics and get really excited. You can also select View list of Ditto profiles from the drop-down box. Platinum IBOs will be able to view profiles for all IMCs in their group. All IBOs will be able to view their personal profile, and the customer profiles of the members and clients they've personally signed up for **Ditto Delivery**. You'll see the **Profile List**, a complete listing of the people who've set-up Ditto profiles. Click on the Profile# link for any one of them to get all the details.

Ditto Delivery allows IBOs, Members and Clients total freedom to access and change their profiles, whenever they want. Which means you do less. While you earn more. Ooh, ahhh!

MARKETING TIPS

If you're an IBO who'd like to learn how to make money now, you'll find lots of good tips in this section. There's a wealth of information here. You'll find pages of helpful hints. Learn how to make money now with some of the most profitable product lines available to you. **Water Treatment Systems**. **Queen Cookware**. **Skin Care** and **Cosmetics**. Just click on the product line you're interested in. You'll find information on **Target Customers**, **How to Reach Them**, key features to **Demonstrate**, **Answering Objections**, and **Service after the Sale**.

If you're interested in making money with the **Skin Care** and **Cosmetics** line you'll find pointers here to help you **Find Clients**, **Prepare for a Clinic**, **Conduct a Clinic**, **Present Skin Care**, **Present Cosmetics**, **Help With Purchase**, **Answer Questions**, and **Ask for the Order**.

MEETING SUPPORT

If you're a Platinum IBO, you'll visit this area of **Virtual Office** to get help with putting together special events for large groups of people. Look here for the latest information on special programs available to you and your organization. Click on **Product**

Education Programs, P.E.P. Presentations, Schedule a P.E.P., Quixtar 101, or **Other Meeting Support**. You'll find plenty of occasions to consult this section. Trainings. Open houses. Trade shows. With **Meeting Support** here to lend a hand, your presentations will be dynamite!

CLICK 17   MY BUSINESS

CLICK HERE TO TRACK IBO INFORMATION IN THE PRIVACY OF YOUR VIRTUAL OFFICE. YOU'LL GET REPORTS ON YOUR LINE OF SPONSORSHIP. UP-TO-THE MINUTE PV/BV INFORMATION. BUSINESS FORMS. TAX INFO. RENEWAL OPTIONS. DETAILS ON CASH AWARDS & INCENTIVE PROGRAMS. ALL THE INFORMATION YOU NEED TO RUN YOUR GROWING BUSINESS.

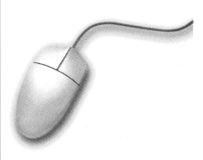

MY BUSINESS

MY BUSINESS

This is one of our favorite parts of the site. It's so much fun to get up in the morning and see how much your business has grown overnight! You'll get really spoiled by having key indicators for your business at your fingertips. Any time of the day or night.

In traditional business offices, most people have to wait until the end of the month to get financial reports on their business. But not you. You've got a virtual business. And your business information is available to you in real time. As soon as an invoice is processed for a product sale, you'll see the transaction show up on your screen. So you'll always know exactly where your business stands. 24 hours a day. 365 days a year.

RENEW

To renew your Web-based business, powered by Quixtar, go to the navy blue navigational bar and click on Virtual Office, then My Business, then Renew. To choose the Renewal Option you want, point to the empty circle next to your choice and click in it to place a black dot inside the circle. Then click Continue. If you'd like more specifics on the different renewal options available to you, look on the left side of your screen and you'll see Click here just below **Questions?** in the small navy blue bar. Follow that link and you'll find all the information you need.

That Was a Good Move When deciding which renewal option you'll choose, it's a good idea to check with your team leader. For most IBOs, this will be your Platinum IBO. They're sure to steer you in the right direction. Just ask!

REWARDS & INCENTIVES

One of the many benefits of being an IBO is the multitude of **Rewards & Incentives** you'll be eligible for as you reach various levels of achievement in the business. You'll want to explore this area to look at all the wonderful experiences that await you. Click on Pins to see the levels of achievement you can reach. Each pin level has a nice title. Most of them are named after precious metals and gems, like Silver, Gold, Platinum, Ruby, Sapphire, Emerald and Diamond. And most pins come with a very nice cash award, ranging from $1000 to $150,000.

Some pins also come with an invitation to a fabulous resort destination, like Walt Disney World, Hawaii, or a private Caribbean island getaway. There you'll learn what's new at Quixtar and be recognized for your accomplishments. Click on R&R to see the upcoming destinations. They'll be listed on the left side of your screen. Click on any one of them for more exciting details. Then, use your Back button to return to the **R&R** page and click on How do I qualify?

Back on the **Rewards & Incentives** page, be sure to check out the **Cash** awards page. Click on Cash and you'll see a page that gives you the dollars and cents for each type of cash award available to you.

Hold on to Your Hats Because there are some eye-popping numbers here! Just remember, this is real money that's being paid out to real people, just like you. The people who do the work make the money. Isn't that good to know?

On the **Cash** page, you'll see three types of awards listed on the left side of your screen. Click on Awards Programs , Bonuses , and One-Time Cash Awards to get the scoop on all the money that's available.

Money, Money, Who's Got the Money? Did you know that in its first 100 days of business Quixtar did over $100 million in business and paid out over $30 million in cash bonuses to IBOs? That's incredible!

And, there's more! For you high-flyers out there, you'll want to know about the Learjet® privileges you can earn as part of the **Rewards & Incentives** program. Click on Wings to read all about the free flight time available to qualified IBOs. We think you'll agree that "nothing else comes close™" to a Learjet®.

MY ORGANIZATION

If you've ever waded through stacks of computer printouts to get the vital business information you need, you'll really appreciate this part of the site. **My Organization** gives you all the information you're looking for to run your business, without piling it higher and deeper on your desk. From the navy blue navigational bar, click on Virtual Office , then My Business , then My Organization . Look for the Line of Sponsorship icon and click on that next.

You'll see a list of the IBOs in your organization. There will be a separate line for each IBO and you'll see their IBO number, name, and email address. You can choose to arrange this list any way you like. Look up near the top of your screen and locate a small navy blue bar that contains the word **FLAGS**. Click in the drop-down box labeled **View** and select the way you'd like to see your list ordered. View these IBOs by Last Name, First Name, IBO Number, State and City, or Zip Code. Now, click in the **List View** circle and then click the gray **Refresh** button. Watch that list rearrange itself right before your eyes! Isn't that great?

If you'd like to see a list of IBOs arranged in a family tree style list, click in the **Tree** circle and then click Refresh. Each IBO will now appear to be connected to the IBOs they've personally registered. Each new level in the tree is indented to make it easier for you to follow.

You can do lots of neat stuff on this page. There may be times that you only want to see part of your list. Like when you're planning an out-of-town trip. Let's say you're going to be in Chicago, just for the weekend, and you'd like to get together with the people who live in the area while you're there. Instead of relying on your memory to tell you who lives in that area, you can use the **FLAGS** feature in **My Organization** to contact them before you go.

Click in the **"Specified" Value** box in the middle and type in **Chicago**. Next, click on the drop-down arrow in the **Choose option from the following list to flag IBOs** box, located at the top, and select Specified city. Now, click in the **Flagged Only** circle and then click the gray **Refresh** button. And voila! There's a list of just the people in Chicago, with a little red flag next to each one. Isn't that wonderful? You may see a little gray plus symbol (+) next to some of the names. If you click on one of those pluses, you'll see the IBOs in their organization.

Oops, we almost forgot to mention that there is additional information available for each IBO. Just click on their IBO number and you'll see a separate page of information, including their mailing address, telephone numbers, and even their birthday, if they provided it when they registered.

You can flag all sorts of information this way. Perhaps you'd like to see all the new IBOs in your organization so you can give them a call to welcome them and answer their questions. This time, choose New within 7 or specified (1 to 30) days from the drop-down box. If you want to see just those who have registered as IBOs in the last week, click on Refresh and you're all set. If you'd like to see those within the last 30 days, or any number of days other than 7, type the **number** of days in the **"Specified" Value** box and then click Refresh.

Other items you can choose from the drop-down box include IBOs with Zero volume in the current business month, those with a Birthday within the next 30 days, those with a Business anniversary within the next 30 days, Group leaders, those with a Specified IBO number, Specified last name, Specified city, or Specified state. Remember to type in the **"Specified" Value** in the appropriate box, whenever that applies.

If you'd like to send an email message to one of these people, just click on the email address that appears next to their name and presto! You've opened up a window that will let you write them a note. Click send when you're done and your message is on its way. Isn't that nifty?

But, it gets better! See that little gold PV/BV icon next to each IBO number? Pick one and click on it. Hey, look at that! There's the **PV/BV** for the IBO you selected, both their **Personal** and their **Group Volume**. That is cool. And current. It even includes the orders that were placed moments ago.

PV/BV can also be displayed for each IBO on your list automatically. Just click in the **Show PV/BV** box in the FLAGS section and then click Refresh.

All the nitty-gritty details on using the features in this section are available to you when you click on Click here for more detailed instructions (FAQs). You'll find this link at the top of your screen, just above the **FLAGS** boxes. Whichever way you want to look up your information, you can do it in **My Organization**.

Let's Get Personal Even though you've got all these nifty techno-features available to you in Virtual Office, remember that nothing can replace the personal touch you bring to your business. So pick up the phone, and give that new IBO a call to welcome them aboard!

My Organization also lets you keep track of your **Member/Client List**. Click on Member/Client List and you'll see all the names, Quixtar numbers, and email addresses for the people you personally registered. Just like with the IBOs in your **LOS**, you can locate these folks by city, state, or last name. And you'll be able to email them with just a single click. You'll find all the details on these and other features at the top of the **Member/Client List** page, where you see Click here for more detailed instructions .

PV/BV

If love is what makes the world go 'round, then volume is what keeps your business humming. PV /BV is nothing more than an abbreviation for the volume generated by your business. PV stands for point value and BV stands for business volume. Both are important numbers for you to keep track of in your business. The amount of PV your organization has determines the percentage bonus bracket that will be used to pay you your monthly performance bonus. The higher the PV, the higher your bonus percentage. The performance bonus begins at 3% for IBOs whose group PV reaches 100 and climbs to 25% when an IBO's group PV reaches 7500. The amount of BV your group has is multiplied by your bonus bracket and is used in calculating your performance bonus. You'll find these, and all the other important numbers, available to you during the IBO registration in **Income Options**.

So, how do you score PV/BV? Well, each order placed through the Quixtar site, whether it's from the **Quixtar Exclusives**, **Store For More**, or **Partner Stores**, has PV/BV attached to it. You'll see the PV/BV totals for your order when you checkout. You can keep track of them yourself, if you want to, or you can just use the PV/BV section of **Virtual Office** to track your volume.

If you're more of a people person than a numbers person, that's great. Let **Virtual Office** handle all the tallying. All you need to remember is the more people, the more points. And the more points, the more money.

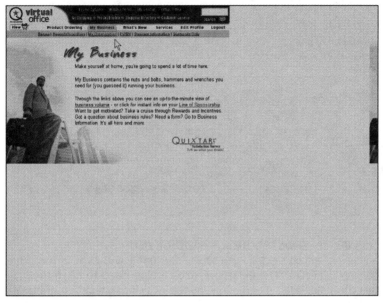

FIGURE 17-1 **My Business**

Okay, so you're ready to check your volume. From the navy blue navigational bar, click on Virtual Office, then My Business, then PV/BV. Next, click on the PV/BV Inquiry icon. Select PV/BV options by clicking in the circle next to the month you want to see. You'll have a choice of either **the Current Business Month** or the **Next Business Month**. The current month is generally the month you're interested in.

Click in the little boxes next to Group Leaders or Pending PV/BV Transfers if you want the volume you'll see to **Include** those items. These boxes are generally used by Platinum IBOs. For

specifics on using these features, locate the **PV/BV Inquiry** icon
at the top of this page. Just to the right, you'll see Click here for
more detailed instructions. When you do, you'll get several pages
of **Frequently Asked Questions** on these advanced features.

Now, click on the gray button for Logged in IBO, that's you! Quick
as a wink, you'll see the PV/BV totals for each person in your
organization. If you have a large group, you'll need to scroll down
to the bottom of the page to see the **Total Group PV/BV**. Your
Personal PV/BV will appear at the end of the list, just above
your **Total Group PV/BV**.

All Present and Accounted For   If you have
a really large group, you may see a message
next to your totals that tells you that not all
your downlines could be displayed. Don't
worry, even though you may not see every IBO
by name, rest assured that all of their volume
is included in your **Total Group PV/BV**.

If you'd like to **View PV/BV for another IBO** in your
organization, scroll back to the top of the page and click in the box
called IBO#. Type in **their IBO#**. You'll also need to fill in their
PIN in the next box. Then, click on the gray button called Another
IBO. Before you can say Jack Robinson, you'll see a list of all the
IBOs in their group, with volume displayed for each one. Again,
Total Group PV/BV for that IBO will be at the bottom of the
page.

There are situations when a **PV/BV Transfer** will need to be
made from one IBO to another. In these cases, you can handle
the transfer right here, in your Virtual Office. Begin at the navy
blue navigational bar. Click on Virtual Office, then My Business,
then PV/BV, then PV/BV Transfer. Click in the first Transfer to
IBO# box and type in the **IBO#** that will receive the volume.
Next, click in the boxes for PV and BV and enter the exact
amounts you want to have transferred. If you have more than
one transfer, just repeat these steps in the other boxes provided.

When you are finished, click on Next.   If you want to erase the information you've typed, you can click on Cancel.

Another feature of the **PV/BV** section relates to **Ditto Delivery**. When you enter Virtual Office and click on My Business, then PV/BV, you'll see two **Ditto Delivery** icons.   One is for **Group Portfolio Ditto Delivery** and the other is for **Personal Portfolio Ditto Delivery**. We explored these features earlier *in Click 16 Product Ordering* in the section called *Ditto Delivery – The Details*. You'll have access to these features from the PV/BV section, too, because they can show you the volume you can expect for the rest of the month, even before it's posted in the PV/BV totals.

See how much information is available in your **Virtual Office**. Why, you'd have to have a whole staff of secretaries, bookkeepers, and assistants to provide you with the information you'll get from your **Virtual Office**. And, there's more! Go Back to My Business and click on Business Information.   Golly, gee whiz! Look at all this stuff. You can click on Business Rules, Tax Information, Business Forms, Information on how to run your business, and Legal bulletin. Just think about how many filing cabinets you'll save by not having to have all this information cluttering up your office.

Let's take a look at some of the areas. **Business Rules** is a good reference source for topics like Definitions, Becoming an IBO, Responsibilities and Obligations of IBOs and sponsors, Preservation of Lines of Sponsorship, Business Support Materials, Presentation of the IBO Plan, Trade names, trademarks and copyrights, Death and Inheritance, Dispute resolution procedures and Enforcement of the rules. Click on any of these topics for detailed information on that subject.

Tax Information includes three sections: **U.S. Income Taxes**, **State Sales Taxes**, and **Sales Tax Forms**. Each of these topics has a drop-down box that you can click on to select specific topics of interest to you. Here, you'll find **Sales Tax Rates** for each State. You can even print out **Sales Tax Forms** using Adobe® Acrobat® Reader. If you need a copy of this software, you can download it for free from the link on this page.

Business Forms contains some handy forms that IBOs need from time to time in their business. Click on this selection to get a list of all the forms that are available for you to download using Adobe® Acrobat® Reader. Anyone needing this software can click on the gold box and download it at no charge.

Go on Back to the Business Information page and click on Information on how to run your business. This will take you to a page called **Best Practices FAQ**. Here, you'll find answers to all kinds of questions, including how you can create a personal IBO Website to promote your business. If you need legal information, use your Back button to get to the Legal Bulletin page. Here, you'll find a wide range of information on legal issues relating to the operation of independent businesses. If you're at all like us, you'll probably save all that information for reference purposes, like when you have to look up a specific issue that's important to you.

And if it's important to you, chances are, it's also important to somebody else. So feel free to email the folks at QUIXTAR.com℠ with your requests for things you'd like to see added to the site. It just gets better and better with each passing day. And so do you! Remember, the best is yet to come!

INDEX

A

Achievers, 153
address change, 22
Adobe® Acrobat® Reader,
83, 163, 175
allergies, 36, 47, 93, 120
Alphabetical Listing, 14,
26
Amvox, 154
Anchor Stores, 75
anti-aging products, 50, 57
Antioxidants, 47
Archive, 33, 45, 51
Aromatherapy, 50, 57, 58
asthma, 36, 93, 120
Auto Network, 154
Automotive, 13, 25, 67, 143
Awards Programs, 169
A-Z Index, 14, 88, 92

B

Baby, 13, 25, 67
Back button, 38, 82
Back Orders, 69
Bank Draft, 70
Beauty, 13, 25, 49, 51, 66

bonuses, 30, 169, 172
Browser, 4, 38
business support materials,
153, 156

C

Canadian, 10, 140
Cancel Order, 19, 41
case lots, 162
Catalog City, 84
Catalogs Tab, 86, 88, 92
Category Listing, 13, 86, 88
CD-ROMs, 68
checkout, 19, 28, 29, 38, 40,
69, 88
Christmas Catalog, 68
Cleaners, 30, 36, 66
ClickMiles™, 140, 146
ClickRewards™, 139, 146
Client, i, 8, 133, 160, 165
Client registration, 7
Clothing, 86
Continue shopping, 88
Continue to Checkout, 146
cookies, 19, 144
Cooking Club, 32, 36
Cookware, 30, 36, 144, 165

Cosmetics, i, 30, 49, 51, 52, 57, 165
coupons, 88
credit card, 19, 41, 70, 88
Crystal, 30, 36, 144
Customer Service, iii, 10, 16, 18, 21, 69, 70, 155
Cutlery, 30, 36, 165

D

Delete, 9, 38, 39, 137
delivery, 30, 40, 160
discount stores, 18
Diseases and Conditions, 47
Disinfectants, 30, 36
Disney World, 17, 168
Ditto Delivery, 11, 15, 16, 28, 30, 153, 158, 163, 175
Ditto Delivery Portfolio, 164
Ditto Delivery Profile, 159, 164
Ditto Delivery Schedule, 161, 163
download, 53, 144

E

eaches, 162
e-commerce, i, 21
Electronics, 13, 25, 66
email, 21, 40, 70, 150, 155, 170, 171
Entertainment, 86
Environmental   Protection Agency, 36
exchanges, 20, 21, 146
Expert Advice, ii, 33, 45, 51

F

FAQ, 16, 17, 19, 33, 45, 51, 146, 153, 159, 174, 176
Fashion, 13, 14, 25, 30, 65
First Alert, 42, 77
Flags, 170
Food, 13, 25, 30, 66, 71
Forms, Business, 175, 176
Fragrance, 68
FranklinCovey, 42
Frequent Flyer Miles, 139, 144
front door, 6, 15
FRY MULTIMEDIA, i

G

Gardening, 13, 25, 86
Gateway® computer systems, 154
Getting Started, 16, 159
gift cards, 88
gift certificates, 88
Gift Registry, 87
Gifts, 13, 25, 30, 36, 71
Go Shopping, 15, 23, 24, 36, 160
Guarantee, 7, 19, 20, 21, 24, 52, 69, 86, 141
guest, 7, 8

H

Hair Care, 30, 49, 56
Health, 25, 43
Help, 16, 18, 21, 24, 69, 86, 165
high-tech, 21, 160
high-touch, 21, 160
Hint, 10, 21, 149
History, 47, 134, 135, 164
Home Care, 13, 25

Home Page, 6, 15, 69, 86, 90, 142
Hot Buys, 11, 28, 30, 31, 59, 68
Hotspots, 11
Housewares, 13, 25

I

IBM, i, 78
IBO, i, 39, 40, 149, 168
IBO cost, 162
IBO Registration, 133, 148
IBO Web Site, 176
icon, ii, 28
IMC, 74
IMC#, 160
Incentives, 168
Income Options, 147
Insurance, 42, 143
International, 10, 19
Internet Service, 42
Invoice #, 70, 150, 164
ISP, 5

J

Janitorial, 68
Jewelry, 68
Johns Hopkins Health Information, 47

K

key, iii, 7, 148

L

Laundry, 30, 33, 34, 35, 36, 67
Leisure, 13, 25, 72
Line of Sponsorship, 153, 170

Lingo, ii, 4, 5, 17, 18, 19, 20, 28, 52, 53, 61, 82
link, i, 19, 47, 69
Log-In, ii, 18
Log-Out, 155

M

Magnets, 30, 48
Maps, 133, 135
MCI WorldCom, 42, 79
Member, i, 7, 11, 133, 139, 140, 142, 143, 146
Member Registration, 143, 144
MICROSOFT, i, iii
More Info, 37, 61
Mortgage Services, 42
Multi-Line Form, 14, 25, 157
My Assessment, 19, 45, 47, 51
My Business, 167
My Health, 11, 28, 30, 43, 44, 45
My Home, 11, 28, 30, 32, 36
My Organization, 169
My Quixtar, 132
My Self, 11, 28, 30, 49

N

Navigation Tips, 16
navigational bar, 82, 86
Network Savings Partners, 133, 137, 138, 143
News, 133, 134
Not registered yet?, 7
NSF Certification, 36
Nutrilite, 46
nutrition, 43, 44, 46

O

Office, 13, 22, 25, 51, 67, 68, 71, 80, 152
Online Survey, 11
Order confirmation, 70, 150
Order History, 21, 70, 164
Order Preview, 40, 70, 146
Order, How to, 19, 156
Ordering Help, 39

P

pain, 45, 48
Partner Store, ii, 8, 11, 19, 21, 29, 31, 71
password, 7, 9, 16, 18, 21, 22, 85, 88, 143, 144, 149, 155
payment, 19, 41, 70, 88, 143
Performance Food, 30, 48
Personal Products, 13, 25
Personal Shoppers® **Catalog**, 68
Pets, 13, 25, 66
phone numbers, toll-free, 21, 69, 138
Physician Referrals, 47
Pins, 168
Placing An Order, 16
Platinum IBO, 165, 168, 173
portal, 6
prices, 38, 39, 44, 138, 141, 143, 162
Privacy Policy, 11, 19, 86, 144, 150
Product Education Programs, 166
product index, 14, 26
Product Ordering, 156

Product Ordering, phone, 21
Products, 153
Products Tab, 86
Profile #, 160, 161, 164, 165
Profile, Edit, 22, 133, 135, 136, 154
Profile, My Quixtar, 137
Profile, Personal, 16, 19
Profile, PV/BV, 133, 138
PV, 13, 31, 42, 54, 61, 63, 72, 74, 75, 81, 82, 133, 138, 153, 171, 172
PV/BV Inquiry, 153, 173
PV/BV Transfer, 153, 173

Q

Q-Credits, 31, 72, 74, 75, 81, 133, 139, 140, 142, 143, 144, 145, 146
Quick Links, 153
Quick List, 75, 81
Quick Order, 14, 24, 153, 157
QuickTip, ii, 13, 18, 20, 21, 29, 33, 35, 37, 38, 41, 52, 68, 73, 81, 82, 149, 161, 174
QuixNet, 42, 80
Quixtar Exclusives, 11, 20, 28, 30, 31, 37, 48
Quixtar News, 135
Quixtar number, 7, 10, 143, 172
Quixtar Pledge, 19, 150

R

Realty Services, 42
Recipes, 36
Redemption Center, 139, 144

Reference Desk, 46
Referring IBO, 143, 148
refunds, 20
Registration, 8, 21, 85, 144
Registration, Client, 7
Registration, IBO, 148, 150
Registration, Member, 143
Renewal, 21, 168
returns, 19, 20, 21, 69
Rewards, 133, 139, 140, 142, 168
Rewards Brochure, 83

S

scroll, 61
Search, 15, 25
search box, 14, 18, 38, 46, 91
Search Tips, 16, 18
security, 7, 19, 42, 71, 77, 144
Services, 13, 25, 30, 42, 143, 153, 154
Ship to Another IBO, 40, 70
shipping, 19, 40, 69, 70, 88, 160
shopping cart, 19, 28, 29, 34, 35, 37, 38, 69, 87
Shopping Directory, 12, 14, 25
shopping list, 55
shopping mall, i, 12, 28, 71
Site Map, 11, 16, 18
Site Status, 11
Skin Care, 30, 49, 56, 57, 165
SKU number, 161
Special Offers, 11, 32, 33, 50, 68, 82

Sports, 13, 25, 71, 133
Spring/Summer Catalog, 67, 68
SSL Encryption, 20
stain removal, 34, 35
STAR, 154
stock number, 18, 38, 161
Stock Quotes, 133, 136
Store For More, 11, 20, 28, 30, 63, 65, 66

T

Tableware, 30, 36
tdah!, i
Technical Support, 21
Terms of Use, 11
Tips & Tricks, ii, 11, 16
toll-free phone numbers, 21, 69, 138
Toys, 13, 25, 67
Travel, 86, 143
Trim Advantage, 48

U

Update Basket, 38
UPS, ii
URL, 5

V

View Quixtar Intro, 11
Virtual, 52
Virtual Face, 54
Virtual Look, 52, 55
Virtual Office, 152
VISA card, 142, 144, 154
Vitamins, 30, 47
Volume Projections, 163, 165
Volume to Follow, 41, 159

W

warranty, 19, 20, 69
Water Treatment, 30, 33, 36, 165
Weather, 133, 137
WebTV, 2, 66
Weight Management, 30, 48
Welcome, 1
What's New, 11, 43, 50, 83, 86, 153, 159

Wholesale Price List, 163

Y

You May Also Like, 38

Z

zoom, 37, 61, 91